T0271736

Previously published in the United States by Workman Publishing Co., Inc., a subsidiary of Hachette Book Group, Inc. in 2022.

First published in Great Britain by Nicholas Brealey Publishing in 2023
An imprint of John Murray Press
A division of Hodder & Stoughton Ltd,
An Hachette UK company

8

SMART BREVITY is a registered trademark of Axios Media Inc.
Text and illustrations copyright © Axios Media Inc.
Photography within illustrations copyright © Getty Images and
their respective photographers.
Jacket design by Paul Sahre
Interior design by Lisa Hollander
Illustrations by: Aïda Amer (pages: 11, 42, 72, 80, 104, 112, 128, 143, 148, 166, 172, 184, 202); Rae Cook (pages: 130, 134, 150, 154, 158, 165, 188, 211); Sarah Grillo (pages: iv, 1, 3, 18, 34, 56, 64, 74, 88, 96, 138, 156, 178, 181, 182, 194, 212); Megan Robinson (pages: 6, 14, 16, 26, 38, 49, 50, 59, 71, 76, 82, 91, 108, 115, 117, 120, 175).

A CIP catalogue record for this title is available from the British Library

Hardback ISBN 978 1 3998 0964 1
eBook ISBN 978 1 3998 0966 5

Printed and bound in Great Britain by Clays Ltd, Elcograf S.p.A.

John Murray Press policy is to use papers that are natural, renewable and recyclable products and made from wood grown in sustainable forests. The logging and manufacturing processes are expected to conform to the environmental regulations of the country of origin.

John Murray Press
Carmelite House
50 Victoria Embankment
London EC4Y 0DZ

www.nicholasbrealey.com

Jim VandeHei, Mike Allen and Roy Schwartz

Smart Brevity

THE POWER OF SAYING MORE WITH LESS

SMART BREVITY COUNT: 27,291 words 104 minutes

NICHOLAS BREALEY
PUBLISHING

London • Boston

Contents

PART 3
SMART BREVITY IN ACTION

The Fog of Words

SMART BREVITY COUNT:

| 969 WORDS | 3 ½ MINUTES |

Never in the history of humanity have we vomited more words in more places with more velocity.

WHY IT MATTERS: This new and exhausting phenomenon has jammed our inboxes, paralyzed workplaces, clogged our minds—and inspired us to create Smart Brevity . . . and to write this book.

Be honest: You're a prisoner to words. Writing them. Reading them. Listening to them.

- Slacked words. Emailed words. Tweeted words. Texted words. Memo words. Story words. Words, words, words.

- We spend our days listening, watching and reading them, pecking at our tiny screens in endless pursuit of more of them.

Our minds are frazzled by all of this. We feel and see it daily. We're more scattered, impatient, inundated. We scroll. We skim. We click. We share.

- Eye-tracking studies show that we spend 26 seconds, on average, reading a piece of content.

- On average, we spend fewer than 15 seconds on most of the web pages we click. Here's another crazy stat: One study found that our brain decides in 17 milliseconds if we like what we just clicked. If not, we zip on.

- We share most stories without bothering to read them.

Then we wait, fidgeting, chasing instant gratification or just *more*—a laugh, a provocation, a news nugget, a connection, a like, a share, retweets, Snaps. This pursuit makes it harder to focus, to resist checking our phones, to read deeply, to remember stuff, to notice what matters.

- We check our phones 344-plus times each day—once every 4 minutes, at least. Behavioral research—and our own BS detectors—show we underreport our true usage.

- We scan, not read, almost everything that pops up on our screens.

- Mostly we're feeding a jones for dopamine jolts that come from yet more texts, tweets, googling, buzz, Slacks, videos, posts. *Click. Click. Click . . .*

WHAT SCIENCE AND DATA TELL US:

There is actually little evidence that this behavior is
rewiring our adult brains. Rather, we've always been
prone to distraction. It's just that now we are getting
slapped silly with an explosion of minute-by-minute
distractions.

- This exploits two human flaws at once: Most of
  us are terrible multitaskers, and we struggle to
  refocus once our attention is yanked away. It takes
  most people more than 20 minutes to snap back
  into focus after a distraction.

- No wonder the old ways of communicating fail to
  land amid this unfolding chaos.

THE BIG PICTURE: We're wallowing in noise and
nonsense most of our waking hours. And flopping over in
bed for little dabs and jabs while we sleep. It's the madness
of the modern mind.

This growing fog of words has two root causes:
technology and our stubborn bad habits.

1. The internet and smartphones opened the floodgates
for everyone to say and see everything at scale, for free,
instantly, always. We all won equal access to Facebook,
Google, Twitter, Snapchat, TikTok. And boy, do we use
and abuse it.

We can share our every thought. Post when proud—
or pissed. Google when confused. Watch a video on any
topic at any time.

2. But people keep banging out emails, letters, memos, papers, stories and books like it's 1980. Think about it: We know everyone has less time, more options, endless distractions—yet we keep coughing up the same number of words. Or more. Written in the same way we have been writing for generations.

This isn't new. Mark Twain, writing to a friend in 1871, confessed, "I didn't have time to write you a short letter, so I wrote you a long one."

- Everyone does this. We try to fake it—or show off our smarts—by overindulging in words. We see this at work, in personal emails, in the professional media.

- We're taught that length equals depth and importance. Teachers assign papers by word count or number of pages. Long magazine articles convey gravitas. The thicker the book, the smarter the author.

- Technology turned this obsession with length from a glitch to a stubborn, time-sapping bug.

The result is billions of wasted words:

- Roughly one-third of work emails that require attention go unread.

- Most words of most news stories are not seen.

- Most chapters of most books go untouched.

The problem is most acute in just about every workplace in America. It does not matter if you work at

Apple, a small business or a new start-up, it has never been harder to get people focused on what matters most.

- The work-from-anywhere reality of a world changed by COVID-19 has turned communications into a profound and critical weakness for every company, every leader, every rising star, every restless worker.

- This problem will echo loudly through every organization because a vibrant culture, a clear strategy and swift execution rely on strong communications in a scattered world.

- Stewart Butterfield, the CEO of Slack, told us that, in a hypothetical 10,000-employee company that spends $1 billion on payroll, 50 to 60 percent of the average employee's time is spent on communication of some sort. Yet no one provides the tools and training to do this well.

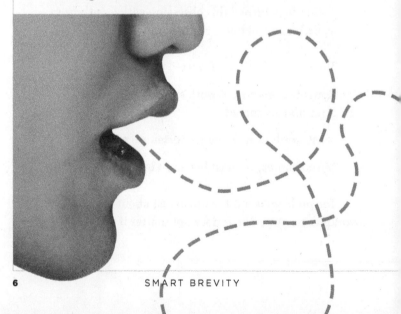

SMART BREVITY

THE BOTTOM LINE: All of us confront an epic challenge: How do you get anyone to pay attention to anything that matters in this mess?

OUR ANSWER: Adapt to how people consume content—not how you *wish* they did or they did once upon a time. Then, change how you communicate, immediately. You can do this quickly by adopting Smart Brevity.

THE UPSIDE FOR YOU: You will learn to punch through the noise, be heard on what matters most to you and win recognition for your most important ideas. And you will learn that this new way of thinking and communicating is liberating, contagious and teachable.

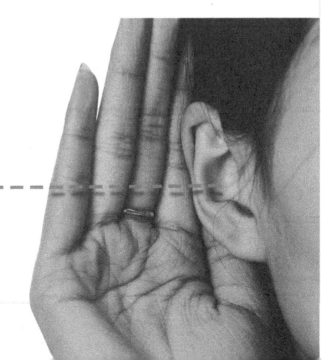

Part 1

What Is Smart Brevity?

1

Short, Not Shallow

SMART BREVITY COUNT

| 843 WORDS | 3 MINUTES |

A lunch-spattered piece of paper hangs on the wall of the Arlington, Virginia, newsroom of our start-up, Axios. It reads: "Brevity is confidence. Length is fear."

WHY IT MATTERS: We run a media company. We live, breathe and make money off words and getting the most influential, demanding readers to consume them—CEOs, political leaders, managers and curious news junkies.

- Yet our solution to the fog of words is enticing people to produce and consume fewer of them—*far fewer*.

We call it Smart Brevity. It is a system and strategy for thinking more sharply, communicating more crisply and saving yourself and others time. It guides you into saying a lot more with a lot less—and that is its greatest power.

- Thanks to the internet, how we consume information has evolved drastically. But little has changed how we write and communicate now that people are distracted and deluged.

Smart Brevity attacks this problem head-on. In this book, we will show you how strong words, shorter sentences, arresting teases, simple visuals and smartly organized ideas transform writing from unnoticed to vital—and remembered.

- We'll show you how the data, the consumption habits of the powerful, the modern digital and workplace trends and our own professional journeys reveal the surprising benefits of communicating shorter, smarter and simpler.

- We'll teach you the foundational strategies that helped us create two companies (Axios and Politico), rise to the top ranks of American journalism and become better leaders and people.

- Along the way, we'll tell you funny and illuminating stories to lighten the mood and show how you too can apply Smart Brevity in your own work and life.

The three of us run a media company, but this isn't a book for journalists. We wrote it to help empower everyone.

- If you're a student, Smart Brevity will make your papers and presentations more captivating.

- If you're in sales, Smart Brevity will make your presentations more illuminating—and help you win business.

- If you run an organization—be it a corporation, a city, a university or a nonprofit—updates in Smart Brevity will make your messages clear and memorable, so everyone stays aligned and inspired.

- If you're anyone trying to communicate important information to others—it doesn't matter if you're a manager, a teacher or a neighborhood leader— this book reveals our secrets for being heard.

THE BOTTOM LINE: You can't rally people around a strategy or an idea if they don't understand what you're saying—or zone out.

- With the old ways of communicating, almost no one is listening.

- We'll show you how to restructure how you think. Then, your writing will break through with crystal clarity.

Do ~~a lot~~ more with ~~a lot~~ less.

We get that you might be a Smart Brevity skeptic.

- Most people are at first. Hell, we were. Each of the three Axios founders made a good living producing words for their bosses.

Jim's wife, Autumn, hated the concept for this book. Watching him bang out chapters on his iPhone made his kids dubious too. Autumn is a lover of words—an academic, a voracious reader. We'll tell you what we told her:

- We're not arguing that there's no time for indulging in words, especially in fiction, poetry, love letters or casual conversation.

- You should still curl up with *The Atlantic*, devour a good book and watch *The Godfather*.

We're also not saying to write short for short's sake—you bring more soul and salience to your writing by being direct, helpful and time-saving. Don't omit important facts or nuance, oversimplify or dumb down. "Short, not shallow," is what we tell our reporters.

GO DEEPER: What we're arguing is this: If you want vital information to stick in the digital world, you need to radically rethink—and repackage—how you deliver it.

- Start by accepting that most people will scan or skip most of what you communicate—and then make every word and sentence count.

- Share MORE value in LESS time.

- Put your readers first. People are busy and have expectations of the precious time they give you. All they usually want to know is what's new and "Why it matters." Give them that.

- Change your methods and style for reaching readers. Now.

You will see quick and substantial results if you do.

- Smart Brevity will make you more efficient and effective at work, a more forceful communicator and more useful and memorable on social media. Your voice and words will pop and echo like never before.

- It will force you to rethink other time-wasting aspects of your day and put your audience before your own ego and bad habits when sharing thoughts, ideas, updates and news.

- The biggest beneficiaries are those you're trying to reach. Smart Brevity can save CEOs and managers countless hours, align companies around their missions, unleash creativity and clarify what matters most, whether you're sitting in your office, school, church or college dorm.

MOST IMPORTANT: You will quickly discover a new self-confidence in your crisp, clear voice—and find others listening and remembering (and hopefully sharing) your most salient points. You will be heard again.

Smart Brevity, Explained

Smart Brevity is a new way to think about creating, sharing and consuming information in our cluttered, clanging digital world.

WHY IT MATTERS: Mastering both parts—making something smart *and* brief—sharpens thinking, saves time and cuts through the noise.

- Most people think about what they want to say and then pollute and dilute it with mushy words, long caveats and pointless asides. Brevity is the casualty.

THE BIG PICTURE: Think about how you want to consume information or explain something juicy when you sit down for beers at the bar or catch up with a friend over coffee.

- People want to know something new, revelatory, exciting. And they want you to put it in context and explain "Why it matters." Then, with a visual or verbal cue, they decide whether to "Go deeper" into the conversation.

- If this rings true, ask yourself: Why do we write letters, papers, emails, memos or tweets that do the opposite? We're meandering and self-centered. Dull and distracting. Boring and burdensome.

A STYLE IS BORN

David Rogers—a longtime star at *The Wall Street Journal* and the greatest congressional reporter of our generation—is a father of Smart Brevity.

David was Jim's mentor in the early 2000s and a notoriously gruff, blunt character. Jim, a new reporter at the *Journal*, was feeling like Walt Whitman and wrote 1,200 words of beautiful, meandering prose. He showed it to David. "It's a pile of shit," David said. He then printed it out, grabbed a pencil and revised the structure into how it *should* have been written to break through to readers. He sketched out a short, direct sentence as an opener, shaved off superfluous words throughout, pleaded for a must-read fact or quote then demanded a paragraph giving it context.

Years later, his work helped inspire the Smart Brevity architecture.

- Something went haywire in our evolutionary journey that turned us all into long-winded blowhards armed with a few fancy words in reserve. When writing, our voices turned stilted. Our minds muddied. Our authenticity evaporated.

THE COLD, HARD TRUTH: Most people are lousy writers and fuzzy thinkers.

- We've all felt it: We gin up a smart idea or thought—a strategic shift, a way to connect friends or pitch for a big job. Then we type it up and it sounds like . . . a big clump of mud. Someone else speaks up, says the same thing . . . brilliantly. We feel like failures.

Think of Smart Brevity as a straitjacket on your worst instincts or habits in communication. It's a way to clean up and frame your thinking—then deliver it with punch.

- With Smart Brevity, you won't have to start fresh every time you have something to say. Instead, you'll have a replicable structure to make sure you sound like the smartest, most organized person in the room.

This recipe, perfected over the years, helped make our media newsletters at Axios among the best-read and most lucrative in America. But, more important and relevant to you, it has started to change how the nation's most innovative companies and thinkers communicate one-to-many internally and externally.

- **FUN BACKSTORY**: A few years after launching Axios, top executives from the NBA to major airlines to nonprofits called with a similar inquiry: "Our bosses are reading Axios and love the Smart Brevity format. Is there any way we can communicate the way you do?"

- **OUR FIRST RESPONSE WAS**: We're a media company, not writing teachers.

But a few calls snowballed into dozens. So, we did what any good journalist would do and investigated. We wanted to know why some of the most powerful companies in the world struggled so much with their communications that they called us, a media company, to help.

- Turns out, Mitt Romney was (sort of) right when he, as the GOP presidential nominee, said: "Corporations are people too." They were just as paralyzed by the blizzard of words as all of us were. Only on a much larger scale.

They too were drowning in texts, emails and company messages, wholly unclear who was reading what and why. No wonder study after study showed employees feeling lost, disconnected, confused.

If you see everything, you remember nothing.

SMART BREVITY'S CORE 4

Smart Brevity, in written form, has four main parts, all easy to learn and put into practice—and then teach. They don't apply in every circumstance but will help you begin to get your mind around the shifts you need to make.

① A muscular "tease":
Whether in a tweet, headline or email subject line, you need six or fewer strong words to yank someone's attention away from Tinder or TikTok.

② *One* strong first sentence, or "lede":
Your opening sentence should be the most memorable—tell me something I don't know, would want to know, should know. Make this sentence as direct, short and sharp as possible.

①
A muscular "tease"

②
One strong first sentence, or "lede"

1:46
◀ Outlook

AA   🔒 axios.com   ↻

AXIOS   Q ☰

Mar 24, 2022 - Economy & Business

○ Your CEO has no lunch buddy

Erica Pandey, author of Axios @Work

f   🐦   in   ✉

Illustration: Aïda Amer/Axios

○ Offices are opening up, but only the executives want to go in to work.

Why it matters: There's an executive-

<   >   ⬆   📖   ⬚

❸ Context, or "Why it matters":

We're all faking it. Mike and I learned this speaking to Fortune 500 CEOs. We all know a lot about a little. We're too ashamed or afraid to ask, but we almost always need you to explain why your new fact, idea or thought matters.

❹ The *choice* to learn more, or "Go deeper":

Don't force someone to read or hear more than they want. Make it their decision. If they decide "yes," what follows should be truly worth their time.

And then try to do all of this on one screen of a phone, regardless of what it is. Voilà . . . Smart Brevity.

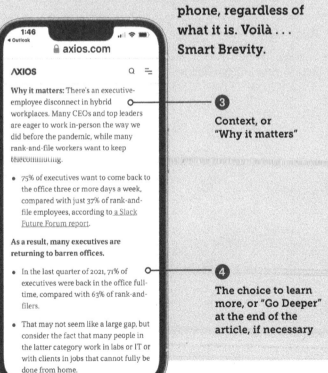

1:46
◀ Outlook

🔒 axios.com

ΛXIOS Q

Why it matters: There's an executive-employee disconnect in hybrid workplaces. Many CEOs and top leaders are eager to work in-person the way we did before the pandemic, while many rank-and-file workers want to keep telecommuting.

● 75% of executives want to come back to the office three or more days a week, compared with just 37% of rank-and-file employees, according to a Slack Future Forum report.

As a result, many executives are returning to barren offices.

● In the last quarter of 2021, 71% of executives were back in the office full-time, compared with 63% of rank-and-filers.

● That may not seem like a large gap, but consider the fact that many people in the latter category work in labs or IT or with clients in jobs that cannot fully be done from home.

❸
Context, or
"Why it matters"

❹
The choice to learn
more, or "Go Deeper"
at the end of the
article, if necessary

So, we took all the learnings from writing hundreds of thousands of stories and created an artificial intelligence-powered tool to help others communicate in Smart Brevity.

- The technology is called Axios HQ. It helps teach Smart Brevity to anyone looking to vastly improve how they write and communicate.

- It has helped transform how hundreds of big organizations such as the NFL; big companies such as Roku; politicians such as the Austin, Texas, mayor; school systems and Realtors connect with staff, constituents and buyers. They often see two or three times the engagement when they use Axios HQ, so we will share several case studies throughout the book to help you put this tool into action yourself (go deeper at SmartBrevity.com).

SMART JAZZ

In this book, you'll notice occasional deviations from the Smart Brevity formula.

WHY IT MATTERS: These are guardrails, not hard-and-fast, never-break-them rules.

If you live by Smart Brevity, your communications will instantly be more memorable and powerful. But your aim is to inform, captivate, motivate a particular audience. Just as a human conversation doesn't always follow the same arc, sometimes you might add a sentence of intrigue before your punchline, the "Why it matters."

- The gold standard is always what's best for the audience—the structure that is clearest and most efficient for a reader whose attention is being pulled in a million ways.

THE BOTTOM LINE: Smart Brevity is music theory—it gives you logic and elegance. But that magnificent architecture leaves room for . . . jazz.

THE CIA HUNT FOR BREVITY

The CIA had a problem.

The agency's analysts were sitting on some of the most interesting intelligence in the world. But many of them were hiding the most important new facts or threats in a haze of words.

This was during President Trump's administration, and the agency knew that its "First Customer" had the attention span of a flea.

For a secret agency, the CIA has a lot of writers, enough to fill a theater, which is where Mike found himself back in 2019. He'd been asked to talk to the crowd about his favorite tricks for figuring out what's truly interesting in a pile of data.

- His tip, which works every time: Ask the author of the data what's the most interesting thing about it. They *know* what it is—and they'll tell you.

- But if you ask them to write a report about it, they'll either bury it or, more likely, leave it out.

The CIA puts together the ultimate newsletter— the President's Daily Brief (PDB), a rough outline for each day's Oval Office intelligence briefing. Philip Dufresne, a former author of the PDB who now works for us at Axios putting Smart Brevity into practice, would rewrite a hypothetical CIA memo as follows:

BEFORE	AFTER
Here's how the CIA might write a warning about Afghanistan:	Here's the Smart Brevity take on the same insight:
ANSF on verge of collapse, threat level up	**WARNING:**
	🪖 TALIBAN SURGE
Afghan government and security officials are discussing evacuation plans, according to [intel attributed here], indicating that most ANSF in the region are not planning any organized resistance to the coming offensive. A surge in activity and violence should be expected.	Taliban militants have been quiet, but our Kabul sources detect movement of troops and ammo, suggesting tensions will soon spiral to violence.
The Taliban seized three more provincial capitals overnight before establishing roadblocks on all sides of Kabul, and now threaten to take control of the capital within days, increasing risk level, our sources in the region report. The quality of intel is high.	**WHY IT MATTERS:** US citizens in Kabul need to be more vigilant, and the US-trained Afghan military needs to be ready to stop drilling and start fighting. Threat level: rising.

EXAMPLE #1

TEASE

BEFORE	AFTER
Hey, there are some new plans for the weekend to discuss re: birthday party	🎉 New plan: trampoline park

FIRST SENTENCE

BEFORE	AFTER
Sorry for the late change of plans but there's been so much chaos in pulling Jimmy's party together especially with the weather this past week. The good news is we found a place to take all of the kids, that new trampoline park. We will do this Saturday at noon.	We're moving Jimmy's party to the new trampoline park this Saturday at noon.

WHY IT MATTERS

BEFORE	AFTER
The only hitch is it's a little farther than we originally planned. The first spot we were looking at was a 30-minute drive, but the trampoline park has a lot more space, so we picked it even though it's about 40 minutes away. Just flagging for planning purposes.	It's about a 40-minute drive, so you might need to leave a little earlier than we first thought.

GO DEEPER

BEFORE	AFTER
The place is located at 1100 Wilson Street by that sushi restaurant we visited that had those awesome spider rolls. Ha ha. It starts at noon, and our session ends at 4 pm. Feel free to stay or go since we have the instructor and we will serve lunch and drinks. I will stay and read or worry. They should dress to play! Shorts and shirts, oh and socks required . . . see you soon and sorry again.	• Arrive @ noon, 1100 Wilson Street. • Pizza & drinks provided. • Pick up kids @ 1 pm. • Dress to play. Socks REQUIRED.

Smart Brevity, Explained

EXAMPLE #2

Tease

BEFORE	AFTER
Board of Directors Update	We wowed our Board

First Sentence

BEFORE	AFTER
We presented on our progress toward our go-to-market plan in our most recent Board of Directors meeting, Wednesday, including strong product sales over the last quarter within the scope of our beta test. We were able to "wow" the Board with a report including a 12 percent jump in revenue over the last quarter, which puts us an extraordinary 90 percent of the way to our overall goal for the second half.	We stunned the Board Wednesday with Q3's 12% revenue jump, putting us 90% to goal for H2.

Why It Matters

BEFORE	AFTER
Strong product sales will allow us to increase investment in key early growth opportunities across tech and marketing. We're updating the second-half roadmap with big investments in the tech team, particularly on the machine learning squad, marketing, to support Ava's team with our new pitch and positioning, and in some exciting new collaborations with firms doing work where we don't have internal capacity but do have a strategic need to add expertise.	Higher revenue means we can invest in two areas that will speed up our go-to-market plan by months. • New hires: We can add key machine learning roles on the tech and marketing teams. • Partnerships: We'll finalize two deals to expand our skills and strategic thinking.

Go Deeper

BEFORE	AFTER
If you haven't taken time to review Ava's new pitch and positioning documents, we encourage everyone to do so. The new talking points went through a lot of testing with focus groups and reflect our best argument to date on why our solution is the best in the industry.	Our product speaks for itself, but it was Ava's new pitch—tested over three weeks of focus groups—that got it into customers' hands. • Please review Ava's materials on the intranet.

The Road
to Smart
Brevity

SMART BREVITY COUNT

| 1,295 WORDS | 5 MINUTES |

Confession: The three of us initially sucked at Smart Brevity.

WHY IT MATTERS: We struggled with simplicity and brevity, just like you might. But our journey reveals the urgent need for it—and the possibilities of success when you reinvent how you talk, text, work and think.

THE BACKSTORY: Journalists are the worst brevity offenders. We notoriously measure our self-worth in word counts and bylines. The more, the merrier.

Mike and Jim rose to prominence when covering the presidency for *The Washington Post*, *The Wall Street Journal* and *TIME* by banging out hundreds of thousands of words. We interviewed presidents, flew on Air Force One, gabbed on TV.

- We would brag when our bosses found a topic so *worthy* we could write thousands of words on it. We never stopped to ask: Is anyone even reading this stuff? *Should* anyone read this stuff?

Then along came the web. Holy shit—what a wake-up call. The web offered something newspapers never did: actual data on who was reading what. Data has a funny way of humbling you. It left us naked, fully exposed to the truth: Almost no one was reading *most* of our words. We filled holes in newspapers, but they were black holes, sucking in our time and energy. Yours too.

FIRST WORD

Nicholas Johnston was running a brevity factory of his own making at Bloomberg, building the Washington outpost of their fast-twitch news service First Word. It provided Wall Street traders and Washington insiders with short, information-dense news stories, bullets and snap analysis and context.

- It was wildly popular with high-paying readers in New York and DC who wanted just what they needed to know, without all the fluff and background that got stuffed into typical news stories.

- Nick liked to tell a story of the (possibly apocryphal) directive he gave to one of his reporters when Senator Harry Reid, the former Democratic leader, announced his retirement. "I don't care what the fifth word of the story is," he said, "as long as the first four are 'Reid Won't Seek Reelection.'"

The idea was that the busy, high-information Bloomberg readers didn't need extraneous stuff about where Reid grew up, what bills he championed or his job as a Capitol Police officer during law school. They knew all that already, probably from Reid himself. They just needed to know he was retiring—and whether we knew who was going to replace him (Schumer), which could be the sixth word.

Nick jumped from Bloomberg to run our newsroom, quickly becoming our wisecracking evangelist, scribbling rallying cries like "Have the courage to take your hands off the keyboard" and "Blobs of text make the eye sad" on our walls.

- Most people read our headlines, and some read our first few paragraphs. But it was often only friends and family who read the whole thing. Humbling? You bet. Imagine being a successful singer only to learn no one is listening to your songs.

Roy was making similar music in the consulting world. He would help create long PowerPoints and strategy reports few ever read. He wondered, while getting his MBA, why no one ever taught him how to communicate or write to save people time. But once his career took off, he simply did what everyone else was doing. We are all lemmings.

THE BIG PICTURE: The internet opened up a world of possibilities. It was changing everything, and faster than our minds were capable of moving.

- Because of the web, Mike and Jim bolted from *TIME* and *The Washington Post*, respectively, to start Politico. Jim still remembers Don Graham, the legendary then-owner of *The Washington Post*, pulling him into his office to warn in his staccato voice, "You are making a cat-a-strophic mistake." We disagreed. We didn't need printed paper or a big institution to overdose on words. We could do it ourselves.

- We built a big digital media start-up—a new factory for yet more words. Jim's wife gave it the perfect name: *Politico*. We connected the web with cable TV and the public's insatiable appetite for politics, and voilà.

- It was, by most measures, a big success. We cohosted presidential debates, hired hundreds of staffers and changed how people read and thought about politics. Roy, who was at Gallup, the global polling and consulting firm, joined us to turn our buzzy little garage band start-up into a real business.

One big moment turned all three of us into such true-believing brevity converts that we bolted the very company we had built to start a new one, Axios.

- Mike and Jim were on a roll at Politico, writing 1,600-word columns about President Obama that were the toast of "this town" (Washington, DC). These pieces were "talkers"—stories that lit up cable and social media. Some were "read" by nearly a million people.

- We felt cool and deeply satisfied—until the data put us in our place.

- This was back when you had to click a little number at the bottom of each page to get to the next. It turns out, about 80 percent of people stopped reading on the first page, meaning they consumed, at most, 490 of our self-important words. And these were stories many in politics and media were talking about.

- We called around to other publications and places like Facebook to find out if their mileage was the same. Yep. We discovered that most people—casual readers, politicians and CEOs alike—read only the headline and a few paragraphs of most stories.

Around this time, the three of us fought and won an internal war to create Politico Pro, a subscription news service that charged businesses and lobbyists tens of thousands of dollars for news on niche topics like agriculture or health-care policies.

- We started mass-producing long stories as well as short bursts of information, often just 200 words, in newsletters or alerts. Fortune 500 companies gladly paid a lot for this service. Business was booming.

- A few years in, we surveyed the readers, some of whom were now coughing up $100,000-plus a year for it. We asked what was most valuable to them—people who need depth and nuance to do their jobs. Roughly *5 percent* said they valued longer stories the most.

THE EVEN BIGGER PICTURE: This was our holy-shit, life-will-never-be-the-same moment. Even the most discerning, high-need readers in the world were screaming for fewer words. The lesson: Listen to the customer and data, not the voice inside your head.

We bolted Politico and launched Axios in 2017 on the notion of brevity.

- We studied Twitter, *The New York Times* and academic literature on screen time and attention spans. Then we asked ourselves: If we were to build a media company based on what consumers want, not what journalists or ad sellers want, what would it be?

- The answer was obvious: Make news and information not just smart, but as clean and efficient as possible. Get rid of unnecessary noise—autoplay videos, pop-up ads, unnecessary words—and write how our brains want to consume. And build it for a smartphone.

- We would tell readers what's new and "Why it matters" and give them the power to "Go deeper." But if they didn't and read only 200 words, we made them the most powerful and useful 200 words they ever read.

We committed to stop wasting people's time. To liberate them from the tyranny of too many words and distractions. To open their eyes to the idea that less is more, and that short does not mean shallow.

Smart Brevity was born.

Audience First

SMART BREVITY COUNT

| 1,837 WORDS | 7 MINUTES |

The very first—and two most important—words of our company's manifesto can help you too: audience first.

WHY IT MATTERS: If you think about serving your audience first—colleagues, students, parishioners, friends—and not your own ego, you will naturally cut down on waste.

- This might seem simple, but it's where most people go off the rails. We tend to think too much about what we want to say versus what others need to hear.

THE HOLY FATHER AGREES: Pope Francis, in September 2021, told Catholic priests in Slovakia to cut homilies from 40 minutes to 10, or people would lose interest. "It was the nuns who applauded most because they are the victims of our homilies," he joked.

- The pope did what you should do: Start any communication by thinking first of your very specific audience and what they need or want.

Picture in your head the person you're trying to reach. This is easy if it's a single individual, but if you're targeting a group, zero in on a specific individual, a name, a face, a job.

- Always do this before you start communicating. If you try to speak to everyone, usually you reach no one. **Singling out the person you want to reach** clarifies things big-time.

THE NEXT RIGHT THING

It was late 2015, and all three of us were in a bitter, secret battle to leave Politico—our baby, our first start-up. It was getting miserable. We wanted to punch back, hard.

Jim sat stewing in the pew of Christ the King Church in Alexandria, Virginia, while David Glade, the pastor, talked about the difficulties of being good. He told a story about how his kids wondered, with all the chaos and challenge of life, how a person can choose to do the right thing, always.

- Pastor Glade wanted to shrink this big existential question into something more digestible. He offered to his kids nine words of wisdom that guided us through our departure—and shaped how we live our lives today: "All you can do is the next right thing."

Think about how simple, direct and memorable that one line is. He could have prattled on, quoting Luke, waxing poetic in Hebrew or dropping C. S. Lewis wisdom, and he could've sharpened it even more: "Do the next right thing."

- Pastor Glade nailed the single most important lesson of modern communications—short, smart, simple and direct can break through and persist.

- In a note to his congregation in October 2021, Glade quoted William Strunk's *Elements of Style*: "Vigorous writing is concise. A sentence should contain no unnecessary words, a paragraph no unnecessary sentences, for the same reason a drawing should have no unnecessary lines and a machine no unnecessary parts."

This is the opposite of TV, where networks often try to reach the broadest possible audience by targeting the least-informed viewer. This results in dumbing down content and larding it up with general context.

- Don't do this. Instead imagine a smart, busy, curious person at the center of the large circle you're targeting. A real person with a real job and real needs. This person should be someone interested in your topic and likely to engage.

- What you present will help clarify what they already know and what might be new, illuminating, exciting. It will also shape your voice and data points and how you explain to them why your presentation matters.

- Your message will echo out as readers see and appreciate the respect shown for their time and intelligence.

The second and equally important Smart Brevity step is to tightly tailor your message to your target reader. You will truly achieve Smart Brevity when you figure out *what* you want this person to remember specifically—and find taut, vivid, memorable ways to express it.

- Test yourself: Ask a friend to read what you've just written, or read them a few paragraphs. Then ask them to tell you the *one big idea* you were trying to get across. It's humbling, but *so* useful.

- It's how you'll discover that the easiest way to get across what you're trying to say is . . . just say it. Then stop. Your friend will be able to spit back your key point, almost verbatim.

We could end every chapter in the book with "Then stop!" That's the part that trips people up. We hide the good stuff in piles of words. We make people deduce what we're trying to say instead of just blurting it out. Don't be fancy—be effective.

WHY IT MATTERS: You will be a much better communicator when you learn to sharpen your thoughts and ideas, package them to pop and stop blowing words and time.

- We tend to communicate selfishly. When we sit down to write, or stand to speak, or plug in to record, we think about what we want to say, not what others would and should want to hear. Reverse this thinking.

  Consider this in the context of an apology:

- "I'm really sorry I said that, but here is what I was thinking . . . and what you did before that upset me and provoked me to say those mean things . . ."

- Better: "I'm sincerely sorry I said that."

See how the intent of a clear apology gets lost in the unnecessary words?

- Cowards hide in clauses.

Or take this into the workplace or classroom. Nowhere do we disguise, distort and deflect our true feelings more than when giving and getting feedback. Very few people have the confidence to be direct. We tend to dance around tough-but-necessary conversations.

- "You do so many great things, and I know I have my flaws, and life is hard and unpredictable, but I really need you to show a little more effort on the projects we assign you. If you continue to struggle with effort, I will need to put you on a performance plan."

- Better: "Here is one thing you need to improve fast: put more effort into your core tasks."

Or consider simple updates about your plans. Think of all the words and time you waste blurting out your every thought and overexplaining yourself.

- "Hey Nancy, sorry about the shift in plans—life is crazy with all this work and the virus mandate—but we need to shift lunch to that nice bakery on the corner. My treat since I am always switching plans, especially this summer, which has been maddening."

- Better: "Need to shift lunch to the corner bakery. My treat."

Or, often worst of all, what should be simple work updates.

- "John—we decided after lots of meetings and endless deliberation to shrink Monday meetings to just the core management team. You know this has been a source of great frustration for many, especially with the size of the group growing so fast."

Who wants to wade through that mess to realize the point?

- Better: "UPDATE: Shrinking Monday meetings to core management team only."

JUST SAY IT

Lisa Osborne Ross—a wife, mother, CEO and counselor to CEOs worldwide—has a plea for everyone in her life: Just say what you mean, sincerely and short.

WHY IT MATTERS: "We hide our insecurity in additional words," says Ross, US CEO of Edelman, the global communications giant. "Your message is lost, your sincerity is in question—and your competency gives me pause, because you're all over the place."

- Ross runs an international PR firm that uses Axios HQ and Smart Brevity to update the company—and also various departments—on strategy and planning. It is a primary way they keep employees in the loop. She is a stickler for applying the principles to cut through the business jargon and nonsense of traditional comms.

For instance, she mentions a CEO who, faced with shutdowns due to COVID, might simply explain: "We'll go back to work when people feel safe."

Then the legal team gets involved. The communications specialists intervene. Suddenly the CEO is babbling in response and sounds like a corporate hack.

Ross would tell her client: "You just answered this . . . Just say it."

She explains that people "waste time couching it, framing it, conceptualizing it—rather than just saying what we mean."

Her advice can make you a better communicator or leader, regardless of title or industry. "People want direct, clear, honest communication. If you try to spin or bullshit me, I'm out."

Ross says that a silver lining of COVID is: "My time means everything to me."

"We have to be more efficient because work and life now all blend together. And if you don't engage me, I'm going to zone out."

THE BOTTOM LINE: Ross says the "feminist nuns" who taught her in school were exactly right: "Just be yourself." And don't hide in a word dump.

TIPS & TRICKS

1 Focus on ONE person you are targeting.

2 Plot out ONE thing you want them to remember.

When Mike was a rookie at the *Richmond Times-Dispatch*, one of the veteran reporters, Michael Hardy, used to critique competitors' clumsy work by saying: "Think, then type!"

- He was snarking, but it's good advice.

- If you don't know exactly what you're trying to convey, the reader has *zero chance* of understanding it.

3 Write like a human, for humans.

Be simple, clear, direct. Be conversational. Authenticity and relatability are essential ingredients. They help people become more willing to hear you and remember what you said.

- Mike likes to think of his newsletter, *Axios AM*, as a breakfast conversation with a smart, curious friend.

- When we're sitting face-to-face, we have social cues that keep us from being boring. We subconsciously think: I *want* you to like me. So we don't repeat ourselves. We don't use fancy words. We don't tell people things they already know. We don't explain the obvious.

- And yet when we sit down at a keyboard, we do all those things.

HERE'S THE HACK: Talk to someone else (or yourself—no one will know) about the point you want to make.

- It'll be clearer, more interesting and more urgent than anything you'd ever come up with if you sat down to "write."

④ Then write it down.

Write down that *one* thing you want the reader, viewer or listener to remember if it's all they take away. Write that before doing anything else.

- Then try to shorten it to fewer than a dozen words—less is more. It should be a declarative statement or data point, not a question. Make sure it's new or essential. Scrub the weak words and delete any soggy verbs or adjectives.

⑤ Then stop.

If we don't *really* know what we want to say—or more likely, if we don't really understand what we're writing about—we paper over it by saying too much.

- We do the same thing when we're breaking up, asking for a raise, confessing bad behavior. We keep talking. It's human nature. And it kills relationships—and communication. So just stop.

Part 2

How to Do It

Be
Worthy

SMART BREVITY COUNT

| 1,092 WORDS | 4 MINUTES |

Ronald Yaros, a University of Maryland professor, uses eye-tracking studies to capture what we *really* read. He found that most people simply scan most content most of the time.

WHY IT MATTERS: Yaros, who has conducted these studies for years, says that on average, the typical person spends just 26 seconds on a story or update. He calls it "time on text." Anything written after that? *Usually wasted.*

- Yes, that's frightening—but also liberating. It frees you to get to the damn point—or points—and eliminates the throat-clearing and useless information.

We knew we struck a nerve when readers started telling us our style was saving them time and increasing their understanding of complex topics. We put an insane amount of effort into eliminating the NASCAR-like noise and distractions you see on other websites and instead wrote short, essential items.

- We had been reporters for years and couldn't recall ever before having received a single thank-you note, nor did we ever expect one. Usually we got hate mail—the price of writing about politics.

NO FLUFF

Megan Green, a real estate agent in Fort Lauderdale, Florida, says Smart Brevity cuts down on foul-ups, doubt and shenanigans when she's dealing with buyers and sellers, who can get very emotional.

WHY IT MATTERS: When you're selling, success depends on efficiency. *(Notice the strength and efficiency of that sentence.)* Megan says:

- "Stick to the facts. Be polite. The process feels very overwhelming to people. I put everything in writing—email or text."

- "I don't waste time by saying: 'Hi, hope you're having a good day.' It's bullet points: 'Here's how you set up your utilities.' No fluff."

- "I highlight in yellow. When someone asks me questions, I paste their questions and respond in dark purple or bold."

THE BOTTOM LINE: Busywork costs money.

OUR TAKEAWAY: In a world full of noise, people reward you if you respect their time and intelligence. This truth is universal. The opposite is true too: They find you annoying if you chew up their time.

Journalists are often the worst offenders. You might wade through 1,200 words only to realize that one paragraph, buried deep, is worth your time. But reporters are hardly alone.

- Why do you have to flip through 20 pages of a book before it really starts?

- Or watch a mindless 30-second ad before getting to a video?

- Or read an intro, presentation and summary of anything, when all you want is the one or two takeaways?

Professor Yaros gave us an early peek at some of his latest research on what he calls the "digital engagement model," which aims to predict how and why users engage with different types of information.

- The Smart Brevity conclusion: They don't.

Most readers are in a state of what consultant Linda Stone calls "continuous partial attention."

- As a Yaros study puts it: "This is NOT multitasking but a user constantly thinking about the next alert, text or email."

- *That's* arresting: Even when they're looking at your words, many readers aren't paying attention.

And even if a reader *cares*, you may not keep their attention. "Time can limit engagement even with content for which we have interest," Yaros writes.

- The professor warns journalists about "kick-outs"—anything that loses readers.

- The top four culprits: Too much text. Too much jargon. Too many choices. Long video.

- What do they have in common? *Less* is more.

Yaros found that these concepts apply universally, from written communication to online video and even video games. We consume all kinds of digital content in short bursts, then quickly move on.

BREVITY OR PERISH

Chris Sacca—a venture capitalist who has 1.6 million Twitter followers and whose bio says he's invested in "countless" start-ups—gives this real-life advice: After writing your business email or letter, ensure that the first two to three sentences say everything that follows. That's often all that people read.

❶ List the points you *must* make.

Write them in order of importance. The first one is the one most likely to stick.

- **Mike picked up a tip listening to a speech by an executive of BJ's Wholesale Club that we use—and you should too.**

  Mike thought he knew all the secrets of public speaking, but as he waited to go onstage after the executive from BJ's, he heard him start and end his speech with these words: "If there's only *one* thing you remember from this talk . . ." That's a great way to signal unmistakably what matters most and what you want people to take away.

❷ Whittle down your list of important points to one or two, if possible.

If not, write them as bullets, not blobs of text.

- **How do you know when to do this? Think about your own reading habits. Do you *really* study an email from top to bottom or go through a report word by word? Of course not.**

  If we're lucky, we know that from any given podcast, industry meeting, sermon or Zoom, we're going to take away one idea, anecdote, tip, hack, quip, stat, insight.

  That's a win, right? Most of the time, we listen to a podcast or sit through a meeting and don't remember a damn thing.

- **So lean into that. Don't let *them* pick. *You* pick.**

3 Do a real gut check. Is this point or detail or concept essential? If so, is there a simpler way to convey it?

4 Delete, delete, delete. What words, sentences or paragraphs can you eliminate before sending? Every word or sentence you can shave saves the other person time. Less is more—and a gift.

Do these things and people will stop rolling their eyes—or ignoring you—when you present them with a new idea or message.

They will start to welcome your ideas and hear them loudly and clearly.

BEFORE	AFTER
The FIRST soccer tournament, the first of our year, will be held in Springfield, at the SoccerPlex, where our boys will kick off another great year together under Coach Smith—and hopefully win our first championship. The boys should arrive at 1 pm and bring food, water, etc., but I guess you probably know that since this is not our first tournament together. Thank you and Go RedDogs!!!	The FIRST soccer tournament will be held in Springfield, at the SoccerPlex. The boys should arrive at 1 pm. Go RedDogs!

Grab Me!

The most important words you type are subject lines, headlines and the first line of tweets, notes or papers. You need to grab me, entice me, seduce me.

WHY IT MATTERS: Most people suck at this. They write timidly and in long-winded prose. This bad habit is easily fixed. Stop losing your reader at "Hello."

- The next few chapters will break Smart Brevity into its components and teach you how to do it, step by step. The most important step is the tease—the very first words out of your mouth.

THE BIG PICTURE: The brain is wired to make a clear, quick yes-or-no decision—fight or flight, click or scroll, read or ignore, remember or forget.

- The dopamine blast of a great idea or word buys you a few more seconds of someone's time. Every word is a battle for additional time and attention.

- Most people read headlines *only* and blow off most emails. Ignoring them becomes a defense mechanism; missing important ones becomes a constant fear.

- The Axios audience team found that roughly 6 words is the optimal subject line for emails—short enough to show all words in a mobile phone format.

  That gets you in the door.

THE TONY ROBBINS OF HOME SALES

Eddie Berenbaum—president and cofounder of Century 21 Redwood Realty in northern Virginia—has a secret weapon when he's sending newsletters to competing agents in an effort to recruit them.

- It's Tom Ferry, the Tony Robbins of real estate—a motivational sales coach who runs Success Summits and sells T-shirts that read: "Wake Up, Kick Ass, Repeat!"

- Berenbaum finds that just putting Ferry's name in the subject line vastly increases the chance his target audience—harried real estate brokers—will open it.

Berenbaum uses Axios HQ to send a weekly update to more than 100 top agents—and has seen his open rates soar. This has generated more business and aligned his team on the top targets and plans each week.

WHY IT MATTERS: A hot name or brand in your headline or subject line—Warren Buffett for a business crowd, Nike for students—gives you a head start on scoring that *1 second* of attention you need to get a busy, demanding person to click.

Berenbaum has found that *useful* content—tips and training—also helps amp up his engagement.

- "If they click my email, they're identifying themselves as highly likely to sit down and have a conversation," Berenbaum says.

Berenbaum embraces the newsletter format in part thanks to his eleventh-grade English teacher at Bethel Park High School in Bethel Park, Pennsylvania. The advice that stuck with Berenbaum for 30 years:

- Write—then go back and kill at least half the words. It winds up sharper every time.

1 **Start by stopping.**

- *Stop* using too many words in a headline or subject line. Limit yourself to 6 words, tops.

- *Stop* being funny. Or ironic. Or cryptic. It's confusing, not clever.

- *Stop* using fancy SAT words or business-speak.

2 **Once you kick the bad habits, start new, healthy ones.**

- In 10 words or less, write *the* reason you're bothering to write something in the first place.

- Write it in the most provocative yet accurate way possible.

- Short words are strong words. A general rule: A one-syllable word is stronger than a two-syllable word is stronger than a three-syllable word.

- Strong words are better than soft and soggy ones.

- Active verbs ALWAYS.

3 **Read it aloud.**

Confirm it sounds like something that would entice you to want or need more.

GO DEEPER: Picking the right words will determine if anyone reads or hears the hundreds that follow. Think about it: You might spend countless minutes or hours writing something—but give little to no thought about grabbing your readers' attention from the get-go.

Think of everything you write like a *New York Times* headline: You want to be accurate, yet provocative or newsy enough to pull in a reader. This is why headlines are in larger, darker fonts on websites and newspapers—they are *the* decision point.

Your headline—or, in an email, your subject line—is the "Hey listen" of Smart Brevity.

- It says: I have something important to say and I'm going to say it in an interesting way that's worthy of your time.

- If you start with: "Low-waste economy hits its groove," you've lost me. But "Start-ups mining cash from trash"—now you've got me.

- You bore someone with: "Do you have a few seconds for an important update?" But you can snag them with: "Big news: I'm moving."

- A tweet no one will click: "This is a great story and you should read it. Click below." Imagine this instead: "SCOOP: Musk's next move."

There's a foolproof way to know if you have a good attention grabber: Would you read it if you hadn't written it?

- Open up any one of the large blue-chip news sites, and you'll see they're full of stories even their own reporters would never read. And that's writing by people paid to write. No wonder novices struggle mightily.

You would never cook a gourmet meal and serve it in a dog bowl. That's basically what you're doing when you try to get someone to pay attention to a well-crafted thought but lose or confuse them with your teaser.

Headlines

The "before" versions are embellished versions of real headlines that ran on other sites. The "after" versions are the headlines we ran on Axios.

BEFORE	AFTER
The coronavirus variant in California is possibly more infectious and might cause more serious illness than the first	California COVID-19 strain is more infectious than the first
Health-care jobs will be able to keep the US labor market growing—even if we see a recession in the future	Health-care hiring is recession-proof

BEFORE

Why some Americans still aren't thriving as medical bills rise

AFTER

Americans struggle to pay medical bills

Email Subject Lines

BEFORE

Some follow-ups for Monday to discuss later today at meeting

AFTER

TWO important updates

BEFORE

Update on our plans to deal with virus/work from home

AFTER

💻 New remote work plan

BEFORE

Product sprint recap for us to review—some new templates to explore

AFTER

Sprint recap: 7 new templates

ONE
Big Thing

SMART BREVITY COUNT

| 921 WORDS | 3 ½ MINUTES |

If there is one thing you take away from this book, it is this: Learn to identify and trumpet ONE thing you want people to know.

And do it in ONE strong sentence. Or no one will ever remember it. This is your most important point—or what journalists call "the lede."

WHY IT MATTERS: Whether they're reading email, on Facebook or on a phone, most busy people remember only snippets. They're scanning your musings—not reading word for word—and trying to answer two questions:

- What the hell is this?

- Is it worth my time?

STUMPED

A friend of ours, Cliff Sims, worked for Donald Trump on the 2016 campaign and in the White House and had a million crazy stories. Cliff has a writer's eye and is an A+ storyteller. After he left the government, he could go on for hours with eye-opening behind-the-scenes tales.

- When he started to write a book, it just didn't flow. The anecdotes were clunky and distant.

- We suggested he tell the stories to his wife and record them on his iPhone. Then transcribe them. That would be his book.

It worked: *Team of Vipers* remains one of the best reads on Trumpworld insanity.

THE BIG PICTURE: Here's the single most useful tip Mike learned as a young reporter:

- After you do an interview or cover an event, call your editor, roommate or significant other and tell them what happened. That's your first sentence. Every. Single. Time.

Here's another truly useful tip Mike learned from Jim: "No one gives a shit if no one sees or reads it."

- The first sentence is your one—and likely only—chance to tell someone what they need to know and convince them not to move on.

- You have a few seconds at most to share a clear answer. After that, you'll lose your reader to one of a dozen other emails, tabs or alerts fighting for their time.

Our brain knows what's most interesting and important. Then we start to type—and we make it more complex, foggy, forgettable. This is true in all forms of communicating.

- After a big interview for *Axios on HBO*, we pick the best moments by watching the whole thing or reading a transcript. We instantly grab the reporter after the interview ends and ask them what they think was most interesting.

So if you're writing an update to your team or a note to friends, imagine you're talking to them on the elevator with no time to spare.

- If they were headed out the door, what is the one thing you would shout and hope they don't forget? That's your opening sentence.

HOW IT WORKS: One of the media's dirty little secrets is that most journalists suck at writing tight ledes. So don't feel bad: They're paid to do it, and they struggle.

John Bresnahan, who worked with us at Politico, caught the entrepreneurial bug and helped start *Punchbowl News*. He is a gruff, grumpy, no BS journalistic throwback—and distills perfectly what every initial sentence should do: "Just tell me something I don't f@$&ing know."

This is a common—and terrible—first sentence of an email:

BAD	GOOD
"I know you are busy and have so much on your plate, but I was hoping to let you know that I am throwing a party and hoping to get a live band to play at it and might need your help in pulling some stuff together."	"I'm throwing an epic bash with a live band."

Or think about a story you might come across with this lede: "President Joe Biden is relying on longtime advisers to guide him through tough foreign policy and domestic crises, and some Democrats worry that this limited group might be complicating his decision-making process." Yawn.

- How about: "Joe Biden is running the White House like his nemesis George W. Bush did: a small, secretive, like-minded oligarchy." Game on.

Or how you might ask for a raise: "I have been here three years and work very hard and have this new house and car I need to finance and want to discuss, um, the possibility of increasing my salary if you are willing."

- Try: "I know my value and want to discuss a raise."

Or update a teacher on your assignment: "I apologize for being a little late to finalize my topic for Teddy Roosevelt, but I have run into a lot of snags on research because I keep shifting the focus from his leadership style to a more specific look at the efficacy of his environmental policy in America writ large, but I have now determined his leadership style, while broad and grand, offers more room for me to explore, research and write. I promise the final paper with this lens will be delivered by Sunday."

- Try: "I will focus exclusively on Teddy Roosevelt's leadership style and deliver the assignment on Sunday."

1 **Boil down your most important point.**

Remember to keep your target audience top of mind.

2 **Skip the anecdotes.**

Or jokes or showing off.

3 **Stick to the one-sentence limit.**

Now write it.

4 **Don't repeat the tease verbatim.**

(If you used one.)

5 **Hack off the adverbs, weak words, extraneous words.**

Is it direct, succinct, clear?

6 **Now ask yourself:**

If this is the ONLY thing the person sees or hears, is it *exactly* what you want to stick?

Then move on.

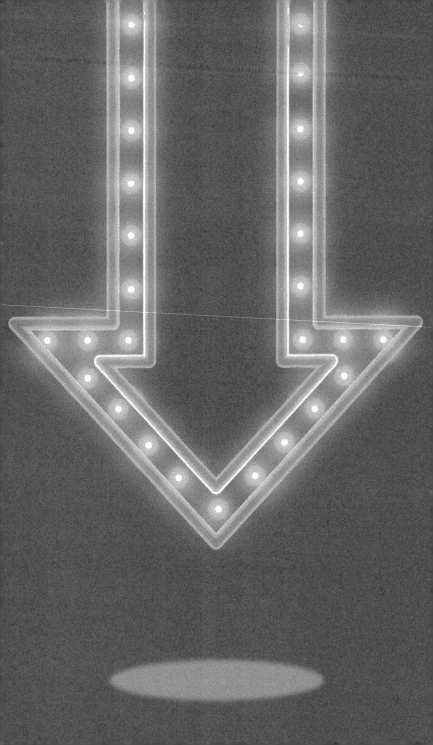

Why It Matters

An "Axiom"—the name we've given to the bolded "Why it matters" headings you've seen throughout this book— is a way to put your thoughts into a digestible context.

- "By the numbers" . . . "The context" . . . "What's happening" . . . "The other side" . . . "Reality check"—these Axioms are all crystal-clear signposts that guide someone who's skimming. (And trust us: They all are.)

WHY IT MATTERS: Most people are too busy to understand not just *what* is important, but *why* it's important. Be a hero: Tell them in a brisk, clear, illuminating way.

Let's imagine you need to tell your boss about an important resignation.

BEFORE	AFTER
SUBJECT LINE: Staff update to share with you when you're free . . .	**SUBJECT LINE:** 🏭 Our chief of staff quit
Sorry to bother you, but as you know, Janet Small has been doing a terrific job leading two of our most important projects. Well, she just informed me that she will be quitting and taking a new job elsewhere in a few weeks. Ugh. Big blow. It looks like she is headed to our competitor. We will scramble to get a new chief of staff but these things take time. I guess I can step in and cover some of her duties.	Janet Small just informed me she's leaving in two weeks for a new job at our chief competitor. **WHY IT MATTERS:** Janet's leading two of our three most important strategic projects. I will step in to handle things while we quickly find her replacement.

- OK, you've told me something new. But why do I really care? Why should I remember or share this?

- Spell it out. Tell readers how to think about this. And do it immediately following your first question.

THE BACKSTORY: We built an entire company around what seems like a simple idea of axioms. Our name is a play on the idea of them. *Axios* is Greek for "worthy," as in worthy of your time, trust and attention.

- Axioms are like street signs: They tell you where you are and where you are going.

- We make the big, most important points start with an Axiom, and we bold it in stories, emails, presentations. It gives the mind a clear cue to take stock of what it's processing. The mind will then decide whether to move on or "Go deeper."

- We basically stole what in journalism is called the "nut graf," the line or paragraph you sometimes stumble upon that tells you why you're reading the damn story to begin with. (At the big papers where we used to work, the nut graf typically fell in the fourth paragraph or lower for reasons we still find hard to comprehend.) We sharpened the idea and applied it to all forms of communications.

A few more of our favorite Axioms:

- The big picture
- What's next
- What we're watching
- What we're hearing
- Between the lines

- The backstory
- Catch up quick
- Zoom in
- Zoom out

THE BOTTOM LINE: Smart Brevity isn't hocus-pocus—it can be learned and taught. There are a few tricks for mastering the art of the Axiom.

Make It Strong

WEAK FRAMING: Here's what's important to know.	**STRONG AXIOM:** Why it matters
WEAK FRAMING: A trend we've been observing	**STRONG AXIOM:** The big picture
WEAK FRAMING: Let's take a look at the data	**STRONG AXIOM:** By the numbers
WEAK FRAMING: In conclusion	**STRONG AXIOM:** The bottom line

TIPS & TRICKS

1 **"Why it matters" is the most common and effective Axiom.**

People are busy, their minds cloudy. They yearn for context even if they don't know it or express it. Bold the words "Why it matters."

2 **After "Why it matters," explain in one sentence—or at most two—why the information in your first sentence is important.**

- What will it change? A policy, a business line, a strategy, an approach?

- What does it signal? A shift in thinking, a trend?

- What's the larger context? Is this an anomaly, intriguing, eventful? Relevant to something you previously discussed?

3 **The sentence—or sentences—should be direct and declarative.**

They should NOT be redundant with your opening sentence. They should add and offer perspective. Say the lede and the Axiom out loud. If they are all someone hears, will they get the gist?

Success is leaving me *wanting more* because what I'm reading feels so new, essential, riveting.

4 **Now read all three parts together: your headline, your first-sentence lede and your Axiom.**

If this is all a person hears and learns, does it convey what matters most to you in the most blunt and understandable way possible?

If the answer is yes, you have done more in 200 words than most people do with 20,000.

Go
Deeper

SMART BREVITY COUNT

| 1,052 WORDS | 4 MINUTES |

Smart Brevity jams essential information into the most digestible and delicious packaging.

WHY IT MATTERS: To master Smart Brevity, you need to deliver depth, detail and nuance more quickly and in more reader-friendly ways after your first Axiom, which is usually "Why it matters."

- Never forget: Most people tune out after a few dozen words and skim, at best, the rest.

- Yes, this is a bummer. But there are several tricks to grab and hold people a little longer.

Giving your reader the power to "Go deeper" is an exit line from a Smart Brevity item that makes the reader feel fulfilled and allows you to point to context without a glob of words that's going to lose the audience.

- As your parting paragraph, just type "Go deeper," then link to your source material or to a video, podcast, bio, map, excerpts from a book, crosstabs of a poll—anything that lets the reader go down the rabbit hole.

HERE'S A SECRET: Most won't. But simply seeing the "Go deeper" material shows the reader that you're on their side, that you want to make it easy for them to learn as much as they want, and it also shows thoroughness and consideration on your part. It says: I've done the work so you don't have to.

- Mike wrote a newsletter item about the ethics of programming an autonomous vehicle. In a worst-case situation, does the car hit the person in front of it, or does it veer and maybe hit someone on the sidewalk?

- Mike gave "Go deeper" links to the news article that inspired the newsletter item and to the academic journal underlying that article. So the reader had the choice: Just get the big idea quickly . . . or read a little more . . . or dive into the nuances of the debate.

Ending your item with "Go deeper" is efficient and elegant—and shows your reader that Smart Brevity doesn't come at the expense of nuance or context.

❶ Axioms rock.

These bolded signposts naturally grab attention and tell others where you are headed.

- **We are big fans of "Go deeper" because it states clearly that you will provide more data and context below. "The big picture" is also a good one when you're zooming out to provide more context.**

❷ Use bullets, often.

The bullet point is a wonderful way to isolate important facts or ideas. Think of how you scan or skim, searching speedily for something that pops out. The bullet point breaks up the text and sticks out because of the spacing and rhythm it imposes.

- **The Golden Rule of Bullets: Nobody wants to stare at a clump of words and figures. If you want to explain three or more different data points or related ideas, split them into bulleted points. People will skim nicely separated, bulleted points.**

❸ Be bold.

By now, you get it—most people are skimming. If you want an Axiom or specific word or figure to really stand out, put it in bold. It's darker and more detectable than italics—and self-evidently differentiates itself from standard text. It screams, "Pay attention to this!"

4 **Mix it up.**

Avoid long paragraphs, always. Stick to two or three sentences, tops. Then try to avoid long blocks of consecutive paragraphs. Use bolding, bullets, charts and Axioms to break up the flow. Big blobs of bloviation bite (say that five times fast 😃).

5 **Just stop. The biggest flaw and time-wasting aspect of communications is overtalking or overwriting.**

- Be monk-like in your discipline with words and Zen-like in the inner joy of saying more with less. This is not natural or easy but can be learned with practice.

- Imagine all the time you will save others—and yourself—for more meaningful activities. This should be your North Star.

- The most useful communication is often silence, grasshopper.

SHINING DIMON

JPMorgan Chase Chairman and CEO Jamie Dimon writes an annual shareholders' letter with big thoughts on the company, banking and broader cultural and policy trends. It clocked in at 32,000 words in 2021—longer than this book.

- **WHY IT MATTERS:** The letter is eagerly awaited among business and government leaders and financial analysts. It might be smart and broken into several key sections, but it isn't brief. Even if that is the way he likes it.

- His staff asked Axios to take a crack at a Smart Brevity newsletter to capture the key messages in his letter and share it with a broader audience. It was a hit—and 30,420 words shorter. (Don't worry, it linked to his full letter.)

FUN FACT: Jamie was one of the first people we told about our plans to launch Axios.

- What Jamie—and his staff—want is for as many people as possible to read and remember his most important points. This requires distillation and hierarchy.

The Smart Brevity version that follows was created using Axios HQ:

To   Cc Bcc

Subject **JAMIE'S VISION FOR THE FUTURE**

2020 WAS AN EXTRAORDINARY YEAR. A pandemic, a global recession, turbulent elections and deep social and racial injustice have all forced us to reflect on the issues that are tearing at the fabric of society.

"THE FAULT LINE IS INEQUALITY. And its cause is staring us in the face: our own failure to move beyond our differences and self-interest and act for the greater good," Jamie says.

- "Business and government collaborating can conquer big challenges—income inequality, economic opportunity, education and health care for all, infrastructure, affordable housing and disaster preparedness, to name few."

Solutions begin with strong leadership, locally and globally:

- Smart financial systems can spark the first step in a family's ability to build reliable, long-term wealth. We must expand them.

- Mayors, educators and community leaders create the policies that empower and advance their citizens. We must work with them.

- Local businesses create the opportunities that communities need to sustain a healthy economy. We must empower them.

- Leaders should prioritize a comprehensive, multiyear Marshall Plan for healthy growth. We must support it.

"WHEN EVERYONE HAS A FAIR SHOT at participating—and sharing—in the rewards of growth, the economy will be stronger and our society will be better," Jamie says. Below, we'll explore ways for equality to win.

Send

10

The Right Words

| 1,067 WORDS | 4 MINUTES |

Mark Twain famously said "the difference between the *almost right* word and the *right* word . . . 'tis the difference between the lightning bug and the lightning."

WHY IT MATTERS: The same is true with soft words versus strong ones, short sentences versus long ones and effective communications versus crappy ones. You want to strike like lightning, not annoy like bugs.

We've rightfully dunked on journalists a lot in this book, but business writing is at least as bad. Don't say "price point" if you mean "price." Don't say "core competency" if you mean "skill." Smart, taut writing is linear, not twisty: Subject. Verb. Object.

- An old city editor once pointed out to us that you'd never call a banana an "elongated yellow fruit." Yet when we're writing, we do this all the time.

- You'd never tell your significant other: "With record temperatures besetting the West and South, and local highs nearing the triple digits, I'm going to avail myself of the nearby air conditioning." No! You'd say: "It's hot. I'm going inside."

- It doesn't have to be this way. There are simple tricks we've learned that can apply to anything from tweets to books.

- Your written work will pop compared to the word salads your colleagues are tossing.

BACK TO SCHOOL

Mark Smith, a middle school teacher in Falls Church, Virginia, realized parents weren't really reading his emails.

- They were skimming, missing key points—then pleading ignorance or bugging him later.

- "They reacted to half of the information," he recalls. "It was a nightmare."

Smith, who teaches engineering at Luther Jackson Middle School, reads Mike's newsletters. So he decided he'd give Smart Brevity a whirl.

- He even puts the number of words and the minutes it'll take to read them up top—just like we do on Axios newsletters.

- Mission accomplished. Smith knows most of the parents just read the bold words (it's not just kids who are slackers). So that's where all his key points go. "By the end, they get it," he says.

Smith points out one area where his 13- and 14-year-olds are ahead of older folks. Middle schoolers love Smart Brevity, but not because of the neurology or psychology behind it.

- As their teacher puts it: "They just want to write as little as possible."

TIPS & TRICKS

1 **Shorter is always better.**

An easy rule of thumb is that a one-syllable word is more powerful than a two-syllable word is more powerful than a three-syllable word. We use one-syllable words in subject lines.

2 **Deploy STRONG words.**

A strong word is vivid, precise and—here's the big one—something you can see. It's something real. A weak word is abstract—you can't see it, touch it, taste it, take a picture of it (like "process" or "civics").

- Strong words: Any one-syllable noun (fire, boat, cage, cliff, fish). Any one-syllable verb (chop, taunt, botch, crush).

3 **Purge WEAK words.**

A good rule of thumb is if you wouldn't say it at a bar or the beach, kill it. These limp or nerd words come in many forms.

- Fancy words: Mike's Grandma Powers used to call them "10-dollar words." You can call them "spelling-bee words"— words that are supposed to make you sound smart but actually just make you sound like an ass. The short words that follow are better.

avociferous *(vocal)*	**conclave** *(meeting)*
prevaricate *(lie)*	**vicissitude** *(change)*
didactic *(preachy)*	**quintessential** *(classic)*
conundrum *(jam)*	**breadth** *(range)*
paradox *(puzzle)*	**verisimilitude** *(real)*
disconcerting *(bad)*	**elucidate** *(explain)*
salient *(on-point)*	

- **Words no human would say:** These exist only in journalism, academia, think tanks and research papers. When we worked in newspapers, sharp editors called these "journalese"—a dying language, thankfully.

discourse *(talk)*	**ubiquitous** *(everywhere)*
challenge *(problem, shitshow)*	**veracity** *(truth)*
posit *(assume)*	**altercation** *(fight)*
dearth *(lack)*	**vehement** *(forceful)*
paucity *(scarcity)*	**disseminate** *(spread)*
obfuscate *(hide)*	**raison d'être** *(purpose)*

- We trained Axios HQ to spot and replace weak words as part of the software, so it's clearly something all of us can learn and do.

❹ Avoid foggy words.

"Could," "may," "might:" Those usually tell you nothing in terms of what's happening.

- "Almost anything could happen." This sentence will do nothing to inform, persuade, convince, delight— the whole point of writing something in the first place.

- Instead, say what is happening: Is it "planned" or being "considered" or "discussed"? Is it "feared," "hoped" or "expected"?

- Any of those tells you something useful. Don't waste people's time with vague, foggy nothings.

continued on next page

⑤ Use active verbs.

An active verb brings action to your writing—it's someone doing something: Roy races Miatas.

- A passive verb is foggier—it's someone making an observation: "Roy is known to race Miatas."

- Active: "The Taliban captured Afghanistan." Passive: "The situation in Afghanistan continues to deteriorate from a security perspective."

- In elementary school, we learned: "Who—doing—what." That simple formula always yields a riveting construction.

THE BOTTOM LINE: Tell me a story. Don't tell me *about* a story.

⑥ Embrace strong phrases.

Short, crisp, punchy = memorable, clear, smart.

"Jesus wept." These are the shortest, most powerful two words of the entire Bible. Nine letters and one vivid, telling verse in the Gospel of John. It captured Jesus's earthly humanity, humility, emotion.

- Japan surrenders.

- Sales cratered.

- Revenue boomed.

- I quit.

- Cubs lost.

7 **Check yourself.**

After you write an opening sentence, look at every word to see if you can say it in one fewer syllable. Every single time, you'll be moving to a stronger word.

- **Never get "retribution" if you can get "revenge."**

THE BIG PICTURE: One sentence is better than two sentences is better than three. Be as ruthless with your sentences as you are with your words. Be even more ruthless with your paragraphs.

Package your words to pop.

A QUICK TEST FOR STRONG WORDS

Mike was on the night police beat when he was sent to a workshop with the late Paula LaRocque, a famous writing coach for *The Dallas Morning News*. She was very Texas—big rings, big smile, big personality. Mike remembers her reading aloud a passage about a fish.

It was evocative and specific—you could see that fish in your mind. Then she asked the workshop what was notable about the writing.

Nobody got it. Every word was one syllable long. The power was in the simplicity.

11

Emojis

Brevity nirvana is saying something with NO words. Well, 👨‍💼👨‍💼, meet the emoji.

WHY IT MATTERS: Emojis, once the cheeky domain of kids and jokes, can be absolute 📖📖 conveying emotion, intent and even nuance.

⚠ It's easy to abuse them or come off like your old man in designer skinny jeans. But used sparingly and effectively, they are 🔥.

A BACKSTORY: Mike didn't touch an emoji for years, on the correct assumption Jim would mock him. But when we launched our first suite of Axios newsletters back in 2017, we were looking for ways to show our writing was 💡 + 😊.

- We wanted to show we took our audience and topics seriously—but not ourselves too seriously.

- One way we did that from Day 1 in the newsletters was to use GIFs as art. Many came from the GIPHY library, which is open to all and strongly recommended.

- From there, it was only a short walk to seeing emojis as a powerful tool for business and casual communication when used wisely, cleverly and—most important—with restraint.

Use them too much and you look silly. But inserted at the right moment, they help instantly signal the tone or topic of an item, saving you and the reader time by getting them in the right headspace.

We know of no science here, though slapping a 🚨 before a breaking-news alert does seem to juice open rates. This is art. Digital art.

- In his newsletter, Mike uses "📊 Data of the day" as a headline—and you instantly know what the item is going to be about.

- Use this 📦 for an Amazon item or 🛒 for Walmart— I know right away what we're talking about. Ditto for 🏳️, 🏴󠁧󠁢 and 🏴.

- ✈️ travels well. 🔥 gets my attention. 🔪, 💥, 🚨 and ⚡ bring you the latest update.

Useful emojis for business communication:

Data or poll	📊
Election	🗳️
Killing it	📈
D'oh	📉
Perfect	💯
Oy	🙈
Deadline	⏰
Restaurant review	🍽️
Devices	💻 📱
Sports	⚽ ⚾ 🏀 🏈 🎾 🏓
Food	🥞 🍕 🍟 🍔

Emojis are also useful for regular exchanges:

- You don't even have to label *this* section: 🏷️.
- Our newsletters signals *Axios on HBO* with 🎬.
- For other Hollywood references, it's 🎞️ or 📽️.
- 🎧 is always a podcast or music.
- And people love the throwbacks: 📺 🎙️ 🎥.

Here's one more reason emojis are your friend: An emoji in a subject line will make it instantly stand out in your inbox. Try it and you'll quickly see the effect.

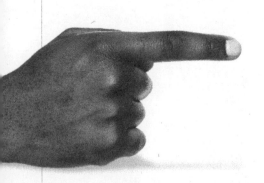

- The *Morning Brew* business email guys have very successfully used ☕ as part of their branding, in subject lines and on Twitter. They use it every morning so it pops when people are scanning their inboxes. Remember: You are in a war for attention, so every trick counts.

- Mike begins his morning newsletter subject line with "☺ Axios AM," creating familiarity and habit.

- *Axios PM*, our happy-hour newsletter, gets a " 🥁 " in its subject line. Drumroll, please.

- And of course these need no translation: 🤯 💀 🍸.

THE BOTTOM LINE: Take an emoji for a 🏃. Your results will be a 🏅.

Smart Brevity in Action

12

Mike's Playbook

Mike has written a morning newsletter every day, 365 days a year, for 15 years. That's 5,000+ newsletters, with only 7 days off over that span to climb a mountain in Maine—and heal from that adventure.

WHY IT MATTERS: It's not something a sane person would set out to do. But Mike's the living incubator for Smart Brevity—his tricks, hacks and discoveries can help you master the art of the snappy modern newsletter.

THE BACKSTORY: Jim and Mike started Politico back in 2007 with John Harris, a friend from *The Washington Post*. John and Jim were bosses and Mike was the on-the-go reporter, scooping news nuggets and building the little-known Politico brand around DC.

- At dawn every day, Mike would write an email to Jim and John with the subject line "How we can rock today." It was a blueprint for the stories the publication should pursue in the day ahead.

- Mike's email followed a very specific format. It always started with a burst of fresh news or insight—journalism's holy grail of "Tell me something I don't know."

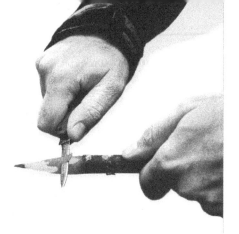

Then it grabbed the best nugget from any hot story by the big papers. Mike filled us in on what a source told him the night before or what party he'd worked. Then he told readers what he was going to do today. He usually closed with something fun or funny.

At the time, we didn't know it was going to be a *thing*. It was just a smart, breezy memo Mike sent to his bosses. But one day Harris was talking to Howard Wolfson, then a top aide to Hillary Clinton as she battled Barack Obama for the 2008 Democratic presidential nomination.

- They were talking about how Politico was going and Harris said, "Mikey sends me this great email every morning, which tells me everything that's going on." Wolfson replied, "Can I get it?" Harris said sure.

So Mike's daily newsletter, which helped launch a massive industry and two start-ups, got its third subscriber—and it spread like wildfire among Democratic and Republican insiders. We slapped the *Politico Playbook* name on it soon thereafter.

Mike's
Playbook

In 2010, *The New York Times Magazine* wrote a cover story about Mike, "The Man the White House Wakes Up To."

- "You don't have to do anything else, just read Mike Allen," legendary *Washington Post* reporter Bob Woodward trumpeted on *Morning Joe*.

- Dan Pfeiffer, White House communications director for President Obama, told the *Times* that Mike was "the most powerful" and "important" journalist in Washington.

- And it was all because of a newsletter.

BEHIND THE STORY: Before discovering the power of newsletters, Mike was an energetic and resourceful reporter, but he was never going to be Bob Woodward or Doris Kearns Goodwin. Crafting graceful prose or gripping exposés was never his thing. He was a lot better in person than he was at the keyboard.

- And that's true of most of us. Unless you're the rare poet in a garret, you talk a lot more clearly and vividly than you write. Smart Brevity helps unlock that natural conversation. It did for Mike, to great effect.

Mike's *Politico Playbook*, which he wrote for 9-plus years, was chatty and resourceful and had an enviable audience—the White House really did wake up to it.

- But when we look at it now, it feels like a hot mess—it asked way more of its audience than was reasonable. It ran thousands of words, was vaguely organized and gave you no sense of what really mattered and why. It was still a letter to a friend—but a friend who hopefully had a lot of free time.

When we started cooking up Axios, Jim had the idea of imposing a discipline on it—just 10 items, numbered, to give a sense of what mattered as you started your day. Jim's insight was that we shouldn't just do *Playbook* under a new banner—we should invent a new form. And that Mike needed literary handcuffs.

Mike resisted at first, insisting that the audience liked it long.

But then he tried a mock-up using the elegant interface Axios had built, with a separate, iPhone-sized card for each of the 10 items. The effect was liberating for him, the writer, and delicious for the reader. It cut his word counts in half.

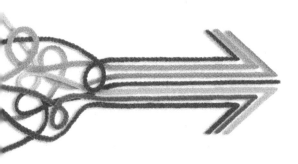

❶ You are the chef.

Part of the "smart" in Smart Brevity lies in the selection. By paring down the selection for your reader, you're increasing the chances they'll hunger for more.

- Writing is like a stacked buffet, where it's up to you to pick and choose what you want.

- Don't make your readers pick what's important! You've mastered your content, honed your idea and know what matters. Just say it—stop cooking.

❷ Brevity is confidence.

This was hard for Mike, like it is for you. He felt he had a lot to say and wanted to include it all. But once he flipped his focus to the reader and not himself, everything changed. And his word count dropped dramatically.

- One Easter weekend, Mike was with his family in a place with slow internet and not much news happening. He said: "It's Easter—no one's going to complain if their newsletter isn't long enough." So, instead of *Mike's Top 10*, he sent out *Mike's Big 6*.

- When he went back to the regular format on Monday, he got emails: "Where can I sign up for the *Big 6* version?" Humbling, and telling.

③ Being selfless is selfishly beneficial.

Once you see yourself as serving your audience, people take notice, reward you, trust you, welcome you and actually read or listen to you.

- Think about what *you* actually read. I know. So why would you force-feed your audience *more* than that?

- If people know you are picky, they will take notice when you shake 'em by the lapels: "Pay attention to *this*."

④ Gamify it.

It's actually kind of fun putting your prose on a diet. Mike plays a game when he's editing someone else's newsletter: He'll trim words—sometimes hundreds of them—and then challenge the reporter to find what's missing. Usually, they can't.

- It's a word diet. Never easy. Requires discipline. But the results are a healthier and better-looking you.

- Our Axios HQ software takes this to the next level and delivers a Smart Brevity score each time you write to help measure your progress.

13

The Art of the Newsletter

SMART BREVITY COUNT

| 1,342 WORDS | 5 MINUTES |

There is no better way to communicate multiple things of importance—and get people to pay attention—than a smart, zippy newsletter, all in Smart Brevity.

WHY IT MATTERS: Newsletters are rocketing in popularity inside workplaces and journalism because they bring order and efficiency to complex businesses or topics.

- *The New York Times* alone offers more than 50 newsletters.

- You can be a hero with your book club, sixth-grade class, volunteer group, colleagues and bosses by busting out your own newsletter—if you do it correctly.

BETWEEN THE LINES: People hate memos, ignore reports, miss emails. We do; you do. A Smart Brevity newsletter, even for a small leadership team or group of friends, demands to be read and can even be a pleasure. Sprinkle in a little candy—GIFs, cartoons, personal news, photos from the team—it's a great way to get known and to instantly make a difference.

As someone who's trying to communicate, you suddenly have FOMO on your side. Who wants to be the only person on the team who didn't see an announcement about a wedding that you placed at the end of your weekly in-house newsletter?

WORD PROBLEMS

Elizabeth Lewis—communications director for Austin, Texas, Mayor Steve Adler—dreams of a world of short bursts of information. But her boss is a word guy.

- "The mayor prefers long form, but that isn't the world we're living in," she says. "We adopted Smart Brevity to help meet people where they are in how they consume information."

The mayor, at her urging, started using the Axios HQ system and Smart Brevity to connect with his constituents. It was such a hit with the public that Lewis is now using it for a city council recap that goes to the media after each meeting.

- "Reporters want the shortest possible pitch," she said. "That's how they consume information. That's how *I* consume information. I want to know: This is only going to take three minutes of my time."

Lewis gets lots of emails that are so dense and obtuse she compares them to the word problems we used to get in elementary school.

- As both a writer and a reader, she says: "Thank you, Smart Brevity, for helping me whittle this down."

Lewis says she has a communications dream: "A world that exclusively uses bullet points." Funny, that's our fantasy too.

TIPS & TRICKS

1 **Come up with a one- or two-word name for the newsletter.**

This should be punchy but clear and capture its purpose and spirit.

2 **Don't waste time.**

Be specific about how much time you're asking from the reader. We use a "Smart Brevity count," but you can simply say how many words and how long to read.

- The average person reads roughly 265 words per minute—the number we use in this book to calculate read time. Do your own math.

3 **Go big.**

Write your first item as a "1 big thing." Start with that in your headline to signal it's the single most important thing going on. Follow it with a tight, forceful headline.

- Example: "1 big thing: We're selling the company."

4 **Don't be messy.**

The first big mistake many people make is not obsessing about the font, text size and layout to make sure the package is pleasing to the eye. Don't spray graffiti.

5 **Then, write a few more items in Smart Brevity, in order of importance.**

- Part of the "smart" in Smart Brevity is in selection. Make sure every item is truly essential, increasing the chances that readers will pay attention to the few things that really matter.

continued on next spread

Axios AM

❶

Enter your email address   Subscribe —→

April 06, 2022

∧ Mike Allen

❷ **Happy Wednesday!** *Today's Smart Brevity™ count: 1,182 words ... 4½ mins. Edited by Zachary Basu.*

📱 **Watch for** <u>new Western sanctions</u> on Russia to be announced <u>today</u>.

📺 *Two masters:* Jonathan Swan interviews Senate Republican Leader Mitch McConnell onstage **tomorrow** at 8:30 a.m. ET. *<u>Register here</u> to attend in-person (D.C.) or virtually.*

❸

1 big thing: New labor power

Amazon workers' historic win last week in New York City may wind up spurring union growth around the country after decades of decline, <u>Axios Markets</u> co-author Emily Peck writes.

❹
- **Why it matters:** Labor's new juice comes as a tight labor market empowers workers in ways that seemed impossible.

A remarkable confluence of factors — including a pro-labor White House, once-in-a-century pandemic and a super tight labor market — helped Amazon workers on Staten Island achieve a David and Goliath <u>union victory</u>, with almost no backing from traditional institutional labor.

❺
- **"It has electrified** all of our members and organizing leaders," said Mary Kay Henry, president of the 2 million-member Service Employees International Union (SEIU).
- **Staten Island organizers** <u>claim</u> they've been contacted by employees at 50 other Amazon buildings in the U.S.

Between the lines: The victory is a rebuke to traditional labor unions, which have <u>failed</u> in efforts to unionize Amazon locations.

🌐 **What's next:** Other large employers are on edge about what this means for them.

- **Starbucks CEO Howard Schultz** <u>said</u> at an employee town hall that companies are "being assaulted, in many ways, by the threat of unionization."

Amazon said in a <u>statement</u> about the Staten Island vote: "[W]e believe having a direct relationship with the company is best for our employees. We're evaluating our options, including filing objections."

- *<u>Share this story</u>.*

6 **Number your items and gut-check the total length.**

Knowing what's unfolding and bidding for your time eases a reader's mind.

- Say up top how many items will follow. Five to ten items is ideal—anything longer is a book, not a newsletter. Trim it.

- Anything longer than 1,200 words total is too long. Under 1,000 is ideal. Trim it.

7 **Grab me. Excite me.**

Choose a cool picture or image that's relevant. Don't slap a panoramic of the Montana frontier on an item about selling the company.

8 **Brevity, always.**

Keep each item to 200 words, tops. This shows respect for readers' time.

- Our research shows a big drop-off after 200 words. If necessary, provide easy links to reports or stories or websites to allow readers to "Go deeper."

9 **Make me smile.**

End with something funny or personal.

- We use "1 fun thing" or "1 smile to go" in the headline.

10 **Simple graphs or pictures that make your point ALONE are pure gold.**

4. 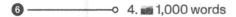 1,000 words

Photo: Chip Somodevilla/Getty Images

Vice President Harris, President Biden and former President Obama arrive yesterday at an East Room event marking the 12th anniversary of passage of the Affordable Care Act.

- **It was Obama's** first return to his former home since leaving office 5+ years ago.

"**I confess I heard** some changes have been made *[laughter]* by the current president, since I was last here," Obama said as he warmed up.

- **"Apparently,** Secret Service agents have to wear aviator glasses now. *[Laughter]* The Navy Mess has been replaced by a Baskin-Robbins."

Obama added: "I have to wear a tie, which I very rarely do these days."

- *Read the remarks.*

5. Bay Area bright spot

25 most dynamic metros in the U.S.

According to the Heartland Forward Most Dynamic Metros report, 2021

Data: Heartland Forward "Most Dynamic Metros" report. Map: Baidi Wang/Axios

We've covered people fleeing the Bay Area in this work-from-home world. But a new report reminds us why so many titans and workers stay.

The most economically dynamic metros have diverse industries, a mix of young and legacy companies, and fun things to do, Worth Sparkman of Axios Northwest Arkansas writes from a report by Heartland Forward.

- **The index is based on** "recent employment growth, wage growth, and GDP growth, as well as two entrepreneurship metrics (the density of young business activity ... and density of well-educated workers) ... and

1 big thing

Why it matters

The bottom line

Between the lines

Learn more

14

Be Heard @Work

SMART BREVITY COUNT

| 1,167 WORDS | 4 ½ MINUTES |

Nowhere is Smart Brevity more effective and essential than at work.

WHY IT MATTERS: You can radically improve your performance and prominence, regardless of your job, by unleashing smarts and efficiency in work-related communications.

- Managers and colleagues will notice—and reward you—for making them smarter, saving time and providing helpful context.

- It will give you a big edge professionally because most people suck at communicating smartly at work.

THE BIG PICTURE: A workplace revolution is unfolding in real time, and it will forever upend how people interact, execute, excel. The days of top-down, secretive management teams ordering around compliant employees hunkered down in traditional offices are over.

This is the dawn of remote idealistic employees demanding transparency and meaning at work. Culture will be as important as strategy or execution.

- Communications will be the central front in this revolution. Those who do it crisply, authentically, forthrightly will win. Those clinging to the closed, cluttered ways of the past will perish.

We talk with CEOs and leaders at the smallest of start-ups to Fortune 500 companies. They all feel the same as you probably do—buried in piles of unread emails, unpacked and unseen Slack messages, meandering memos or company notices too long and boring to bother.

- This is paralyzing and confusing, making it much harder for lots of organizations to see what matters most at the very moment when people are scattered around working remotely.

Gallup, which has been polling since the 1930s, found that two things keep people feeling good about their job and staying put: close relationships with colleagues and engagement.

- Among those feeling disengaged in their job, 74 percent are actively looking or watching for jobs. They're willing to bolt for *any* increase in pay—and sometimes even a pay cut in exchange for a change of scenery, if they get the chance.

It won't get any easier. Jon Clifton, CEO at Gallup, said in the fall of 2021 that only 30 percent of all workers want to return full-time to the office. For those who don't want to go back, most say they would rather move or make less money if forced to return.

This presents a massive opportunity for those who learn to communicate in engaging and illuminating ways. The global communications firm Edelman, based on its "Trust Barometer" polling, concluded in a 2021 report called *The Belief-Driven Employee* that personal empowerment and social impact are approaching promotions and raises as must-haves for employees. A stunning 61 percent of respondents said they would embrace or reject an employer based on social issues.

Communicating a company's values is now essential to both attracting and retaining the best talent. Axios HQ users found that weekly updates by each department, project or team done with a predictable template and cadence helps:

- Align people around values, strategies, a common culture.

- Articulate diversity, inclusion, and equity plans and progress.

- Explain in order of importance the most pressing tasks to be done.

- Update others on progress or changes and keep clients fully looped in.

- Maintain a living library of the essential strategic decisions and thinking.

Our internal research on power users of Axios HQ shows substantial improvements in all of these areas after adopting and adapting to Smart Brevity (go deeper at SmartBrevity.com).

1 **Your messages, memos or email:**

Write essential updates in Smart Brevity. This will bring both uniformity and uniqueness to your communications.

2 **Your management:**

If you manage people, send weekly updates in smart, concise newsletters (see chapter 13). Encourage your direct reports to do the same.

- A Sunday or early Monday mailing works best to align people for the coming week.

- The data show you should send updates in the morning to maximize open rates.

3 **Your presentations:**

PowerPoints are a hotbed for graffiti and eye torture. People smother their ideas or proposals with crappy art and word diarrhea, then hit repeat for a dozen or more slides. A quick fix:

- Start your presentation with your big idea, distilled using the tricks for teases in chapter 6.

- Each point you make on subsequent slides should have a similarly taut headline and then a few bullet points with the shortest ONE sentence possible. Rule of thumb: If you have more than 20 words on a slide, try again.

- Keep your visuals clean, simple and additive (see chapter 20).

- Rarely should you exceed five or six slides.

- End where you began by restating your Big Idea. Then stop.

WIN @WORK

Geoff Morrell, the former head of communications at oil giant BP, was the first person to bring Smart Brevity mainstream inside a large company.

WHY IT MATTERS: Morrell's quick success showed how you can grab notice inside your office, school or neighborhood—and reshape how others communicate. It also inspired us to write this how-to book.

THE BACKSTORY: Prior to BP, Morrell worked at the Pentagon as a top aide to Defense Secretary Bob Gates. He remembered seeing long memos with a short summary up top labeled "BLUF." "BLUF" meant "Bottom Line Up Front"—the military's version of Smart Brevity. Everyone read the "BLUF."
Few read the whole memo.

Morrell wanted his own BLUF. He asked if we would teach him and his team Smart Brevity.

He first created an internal newsletter to align management, and it soon spread companywide. He called it *ITK*, for *In the Know*.

- Axios HQ has trained more than 500 BP communicators worldwide on Smart Brevity, and they have now architected the core aspects of their internal and external messaging around this philosophy. They saw open rates spike—and leaders across countries and languages turn into brevity evangelists.

1. SMART BREVITY IS TEACHABLE. Morrell would tell people to use an active verb in each of their bullet points—and they'd do it.

2. SMART BREVITY FORCES YOU TO WRITE LIKE A NORMAL PERSON. Morrell was struck by the way we send text messages in staccato sentence fragments that the recipient instantly grasps, but our business writing is a laborious mess.

3. SMART BREVITY CAN BE COOL. Morrell became a hero with other executives, who saw the results and wanted to pioneer the concepts with their own teams. Chris Reynolds, the first *ITK* author, became a celebrity communicator, with people throughout the company coming to him for tips and tricks.

4. SMART BREVITY IS CONTAGIOUS. The magic instantly went beyond *ITK* and those employees whose job it was to communicate. Morrell started seeing internal memos structured as "3 things you need to know" or "5 things you need to know." Policy papers on complex topics, which in the past were never read, were now coming in Smart Brevity. Morrell used it to arm alumni and other BP allies with talking points about the company.

5. SMART BREVITY IS VERSATILE. Now you'll see it in BP performance reviews and even safety briefings.

15

Smart
Brevity
Your Email

SMART BREVITY COUNT

1,326 WORDS	5 MINUTES

Gallup, in exclusive polling for this book, found that 70 percent of employees want shorter communications at work.
(Go deeper on Gallup's findings at smartbrevity.com.)

WHY IT MATTERS: Only half of employees reported reading notes from *their leaders*. The rest blow off or skim what lands on their screens, Gallup data showed.

- The way most people write emails screams "blow me off." But you can entice more people to read your work faster or skim more effectively if you Smart Brevity it before hitting send.

- This is the easiest way to win the war for workplace attention. Cal Newport, a Georgetown University expert on workplace efficiency, notes in *A World Without Email* that the onslaught for the average business user has ballooned from 50 emails per day in 2005 to 126 in 2019. So there is a fierce urgency to getting better at this fast.

EMAIL DONE RIGHT: Here's an example of an email Dominique Taylor, our chief people officer, and Claire Kennedy, our vice president of people operations, wrote to us.

- Take note of how they pack in vital details in eye-pleasing ways.

To   Cc Bcc

Subject **NEW HIRE REQUEST (URGENT!)**

As we work to optimize the People Ops team structures for Media and HQ, we have determined that we need to open a new Director of Talent Management position on the Media team as soon as possible.

WHY IT MATTERS: We will break 400 employees by the end of this year, which is well above our original projections for this year as well as our re-forecasts.

- Currently, we are just backfilling roles on the Talent Management team. We need additional bandwidth to support the amount of growth we're experiencing and projecting, especially in this hybrid environment.

- We have to go above and beyond to integrate new employees and to engage existing employees in order to stave off increased turnover.

HOW IT WOULD WORK: Here is an org chart for the Media team structure, including the one new role:

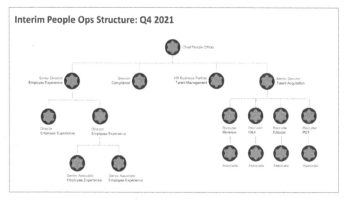

WHAT'S NEXT: Claire is OOO 9/17–9/29 so we want to move forward with these decisions this week.

Thank you,
Dominique & Claire

Send

1 **Bad emails start with lame subject lines. You want it short, direct, urgent.**

The one on the previous page tells me why I need to open the email NOW.

2 **You want the news or ask in the first sentence, always.**

Make people feel like they MUST read on.

3 **Give the recipients the "Why it matters" context.**

In email, this creates a replicable framework to provide the supporting data right after it.

4 **Bullets make it easy for skimmers and close readers to catch the most important data points or supporting ideas.**

5 Bold any words or figures or names you want to stand out—here, again, it's the perfect eye-trap for those skimmers.

6 Clean, intuitive visuals help amplify or bring to life an important point.

EXAMPLE #1

Before Smart Brevity

New Message   — ✎ ✕

To   Cc Bcc

Subject   Smart Brevity training

Hey team,

We conducted our first Smart Brevity open house on Friday, January 31st, 2020, which turned out to be a great success. This particular session was free and made available to our clients who are interested in revamping their current internal communications process. For this session, we invited 16 professionals from 6 different organizations across multiple departments, and all 16 attended.

The training session lasted for 3.5 hours and consisted of 1 hour of fundamental training and 2.5 hours of workshop activities. We conducted 2 writing exercises with our tool in order to help these professionals become familiar with the newsletter writing template. We received some great feedback during the session on what is working and what we can improve on. Here is some of what we heard:

"I really enjoyed the workshop activities because it helped me practice the Smart Brevity tips I learned right away. It could be useful, in the future, to show how Smart Brevity applies to other everyday communications, like email and social media." —SB training attendee.

After discussing more with attendees about our use case and how we use the tool internally at Axios, several expressed interest in having more of their team start using this style. We'll follow up with everyone next week to keep our relationships strong and moving forward.

Let me know any questions you might have about it.

Send

After Smart Brevity

New Message   _ ✗ ✕

To   Cc Bcc

Subject **SMART BREVITY SPREADS BEYOND AXIOS**

Hey team,

On Friday we held our first Smart Brevity open house, a free course at HQ to help clients who are interested in our style learn the craft.

WHY IT MATTERS: They caught on quickly, and several asked if they could bring our training in-house so more of their colleagues could learn.

BY THE NUMBERS:

- **16 professionals joined us**
- **6 organizations were there**
- **3.5 hours of training flew by**
- **2 writing exercises were done in our tool**

WHAT WE HEARD: "I really enjoyed the workshop activities because they helped me practice the Smart Brevity tips I learned right away. It could be useful, in the future, to show how Smart Brevity applies to other everyday communications, like email and social media."

WHAT'S NEXT: We'll follow up with each of them next week to keep these relationships strong.

`Send`

EXAMPLE #2

Before Smart Brevity

New Messege ___ ✗ ×

To   Cc Bcc

Subject   Expensify Policy Updates!

Hello All,

We have officially transitioned to our new accounting system (Sage-Intacct), and that change also means changes to Expensify . You may have seen the emails from Expensify indicating you were added to our new policy, which allows for expense reports to sync to our accounting system.

Please begin submitting expenses under the new policy "Axios Expense Policy." This allows managers/finance to approve reports for reimbursement and for you to get paid. It should be set as your default.

Attached is our special-edition Expensify reintroduction PowerPoint that goes into some general good-practice refreshers and further details of the changes, which are as follows:

- Departments are now under the Departments field instead of "Class."
- Class/Projects (Slide 7) are for tagging company-wide initiatives as well as projects and squad spending.

This allows the company to better track spending by specific initiatives to see if we are on the right track on some of our specific goals. Helping by tagging your expenses to initiatives that are applicable will help bring better accuracy in budgeting for these specific projects.

Business Line (Slide 8) is for tagging cost to our 3 lines of business. This is now a required field.

With the upgrade to the new system we can now efficiently report financials through our business lines. This allows the company to better report on how different lines of business are performing to its goals.

We know this is a lot, so we will also be having a live presentation in early February during the all-staff meeting. We can answer your questions live. In the meanwhile, feel free to Slack/email anyone from finance if you have questions.

We're here to help!

Send   🗑 ⋮

After Smart Brevity

To   Cc Bcc

Subject   New steps to submit expenses

Hello All,

We are switching our accounting system to help the finance team work faster.

ONE ACTION ITEM: Before you can create your next expense report, you'll need to switch your Expensify settings to "Axios Expense Policy." Here's how:

1. Log into Expensify.
2. Click your profile image.
3. Check "Axios Expense Policy."

FOR ANY IN-PROGRESS REPORTS, you'll need to update your settings:

1. Click "Reports" from the left nav bar.
2. Select the report and click "Details."
3. In the "Policy" drop-down, check "Axios Expense Policy."

WHAT'S NEXT: The upgrade comes with a few other improvements—like new expense fields you'll need to use—but we'll cover it all in an early February all-staff meeting.

• Meanwhile, check out the attached PowerPoint for a quick summary. Feel free to Slack me with any questions.

Send   ⋮

16

Smart Brevity Your Meetings

SMART BREVITY COUNT

| 844 WORDS | 3 MINUTES |

Think of all the hours you'll never get back from meetings that were too long, too meandering, too useless.

WHY IT MATTERS: You can transform your team's culture and performance by jamming more smarts and brevity into shorter meetings. You'll stand out as someone who values others' time—and has something important to say.

- The first step is learning how to actually meet. Three out of four people have not been trained on how to run a good meeting. No wonder so many skull sessions suck.

- Other people are just like you: 90 percent admit to daydreaming and 72 percent do other work while in meetings (HBR Design Thinking).

- Now use the principles in this chapter to create coherence, set a clear direction and get better results.

THE PREGAME SHOW: A good meeting is usually determined before it starts.

- Sounds silly, but make sure you truly need a meeting. If it requires privacy or brutal honesty, it might be better handled as a one-on-one chat.

- The person calling the meeting should be responsible for setting an objective (one direct sentence) and agenda (three bullet points, max) in an email before the meeting.

- Try to do this the night before, in case some participants are booked solid on the day of. It gives ample time to think.

- Jeff Bezos famously takes this to an extreme—based on his distrust of in-meeting PowerPoint presentations, which he says are more likely to confuse than clarify. "Instead, we write narratively structured six-page memos," he said in a shareholder letter. "We silently read one at the beginning of each meeting in a kind of 'study hall.'"

- Six smart sentences will suffice!

- Outline the specific decisions or actions to make or take, if possible.

While you meet:

1. Set a time limit: Done right, 20 minutes is usually sufficient. Most people are like robots, auto-setting meetings at 30 minutes or more, regardless of what needs to be done. Shake up that culture in your shop, and you'll shine.

- The Slack approach seems smart: 25 minutes or 50 minutes. Then if you're scheduled back-to-back, you're not late for your next stop. Maybe you can even grab a coffee.

- Test out micro-meetings (5 to 10 minutes). There are no laws or sound theories for meeting longer than necessary.

2. To open the meeting, start with your headline— the one-sentence objective you emailed in advance. This articulates the chief reason for this meeting: What needs to be resolved or debated?

3. As your second sentence, explain "Why it matters" to this specific group at this specific moment. People are busy, often switching topics quickly from meeting to meeting. Let them know why they're here.

4. Next, state unambiguously what specific decisions need to be made. You'll circle back to these at the end with your takeaways.

5. Guide the discussion, setting the tone for focus and efficiency. Think of this as healthy peer pressure. If someone starts on a tangent, interrupt with a smile: "Off-topic!" A wave of the arms can add humor and take the sting out.

6. Be inclusive. Often the quietest people have the smartest things to say. Encourage silent people to share their views too. At the very least, they will appreciate the offer.

7. When 2 minutes are left, bring the discussion to an end. Summarize the takeaways and be specific about next steps. Let the team know that you'll send an email memorializing these before close of business.

After you meet:

- While the session is fresh in your mind, shoot the group a quick email with a list of follow-ups, using bullet points.

- We've found that these emails often prompt people to add points they thought of since the meeting—perhaps saving another meeting.

Doing it wrong:

- Chit-chat and pleasantries are your reward for coming early. (Or, if you enjoy small talk as much as Jim does, your punishment.) When meeting time comes and you're still talking about lunch or the weekend, you're signaling to a bunch of busy people that this meeting isn't that important after all. So why are you having it?

- Too many people, too many topics, too much time. Coworkers are unlikely to say anything to the culprit who planned such a meeting. But they notice— and remember.

Getting it right:

- **HAVE A CULTURE OF STARTING EXACTLY ON TIME.** In the first week after President George W. Bush moved into the White House back in 2001, Karl Rove—who had about as much sway as an aide could have—was late for a meeting in the Oval Office. The president instructed an aide to lock the door. Rove was never late again.

- **THANK PEOPLE FOR COMING AT EXACTLY THE START TIME.** (It's your call whether you try locking the door.) For the rest of the meeting, you've established yourself as the voice of sanity.

- **ASSIGN RESPONSIBILITY.** Make clear who owns what and by when it needs to be done.

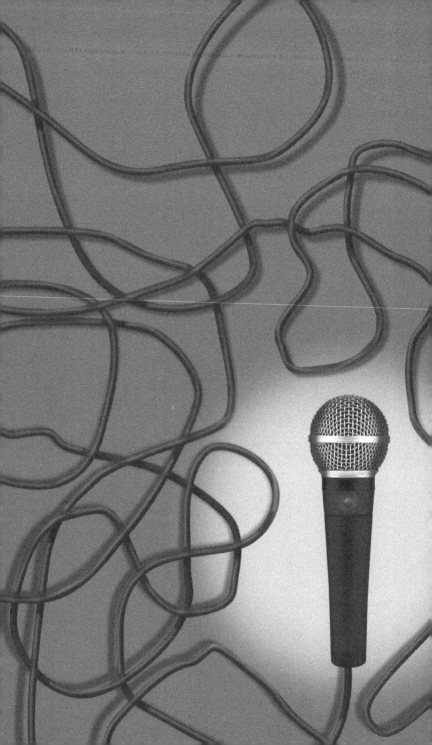

Smart Brevity Your Speeches

SMART BREVITY COUNT

1,453	5 ½
WORDS	MINUTES

When was the last time you heard a speech, a toast, a roast and thought: "That was great. I just wish it had gone on longer and foggier."

WHY IT MATTERS: *Never* is the answer. The sweet spot for a great speech: Make the remarks worthy of the audience's time, and your One Big Thing—your main point—memorable, memorizable and lasting.

In speeches, like life, you don't need to say a lot to make a big difference. Indeed, some of the most iconic speeches were short:

- Gettysburg Address: 272 words

- John F. Kennedy's famous inaugural address: under 15 minutes

- John Quincy Adams's speech on the Declaration of Independence: 3 unalienable rights, not 22

Communications expert Nancy Duarte did a popular TED Talk after studying the rhythm, arc and content of famous speeches, including Martin Luther King Jr.'s "I Have a Dream" and Steve Jobs's iPhone launch in 2007. The Smart Brevity version of her "secret structure" of great speeches:

- Describe the status quo: how the world or topic exists today.

- Contrast with your lofty idea—ideally, the point of your speech.

- Move back and forth from what is and what could be.

- Make a call to action.

- End with a vivid portrait of utopia if they embrace your idea.

Go watch Jobs's slow, seductive unveiling of his iPhone.

- He marvels at his own product, inviting the audience to think about the world as it could be: better, futuristic, thrilling.

- He holds it, shows it, twirls it and describes the flaws of other phones.

- Then he turns it on, like he's opening the door to show you the moon. It lights up, magically and now mythically.

- And he drops the mic with the promise of a better tomorrow—and so much more to come.

OK, now back to Earth: You are not Steve Jobs. And it's doubtful you are inventing a device that will forever change humanity. Most likely, you are simply trying to survive the stage without making an ass of yourself. Here are some practical tips that work for us mortals.

1. Win before you begin. You are a human, so you need to perform like one. Think about writing and speaking authentically. Too many people try to mimic others or speak like they are the main character in a Broadway play. Be yourself.

- Sorry, but slides, notes and teleprompters are bad crutches. You want the focus on YOU and your words.

- Practice and remember to rehearse looking five or six different people in the eyes during your speech.

2. Remember the audience. If you're lucky, they'll remember one point from your remarks. They are likely itching to check their phone or are actually doing it under the table.

BUT, BUT, BUT: Speeches are different from other forms of communications. People come to hear from you on a specific topic. Get the audience on your side from the beginning: Start with a real-life story that hopefully ends with a chuckle. You defeat the purpose if you go on for more than one winning joke or anecdote.

- Here's a foolproof way to gauge how long your opening should be: Imagine running into a neighbor. Social cues tell us exactly how long we can engage them without being a drag or a bore.

- That's precisely how long your opening story should be. Set up the time and place, describe the situation, tell me what happened. Then stop.

3. Distill and sharpen your most important ONE point or lesson. Write it down, word for word—don't hazily know it. Once you have your Big Thought, build your speech around it.

- One thing we can guarantee you with certainty: If you don't know your one-sentence takeaway, there's no chance your audience will either.

- Simplify your Big Thought into one SHORT sentence. Then polish word by word, using the strong word model in chapter 10 (one-syllable words = 🔥). The more provocative, the better. Will audience members rush to share your point with their significant other, coworkers, friends by the pool? If not, you have work to do.

- The *Harvard Business Review* recommends 15 words max for your big point. We would advise the shorter, the better.

4. Hit them over the head with your point. Atop your remark, say: "The one thing I want you to remember today is . . ." Then follow with your sharpened Big Thought, verbatim. You'll instantly have everyone's attention. You're doing their brains' work for them—sorting the gist from the fluff.

5. Follow with your verbal "Why it matters"— short context for your Big Thought. Maybe even say, "This matters to you because . . ." It keeps you organized and keeps the audience on their toes.

6. Then unfurl a couple of stats or stories to back up the Big Thought and bring it to life. It helps to number them, and to announce that at the top: "Five points . . ." Make it fun—maybe say the number dramatically, or with a verbal wink.

- Numbering your supporting stats helps the audience take notes. But more to the point: It shows you know where you're going. If you show you're in command, the audience will follow.

- Or follow the Nancy Duarte model of showing the radical differences between life before and life after implementing your idea.

- Either way, a logical, easy-to-follow arc is essential. And keep your ideas and examples simple and relatable; complexity is a total buzzkill.

7. Reinforce your Big Thought at the end by saying: "Remember, if there is one thing you take away . . ."

And say thank you. Always end everything on a gracious, grateful note. It makes people want to cheer for you.

DOING IT WRONG: Maybe President Joe Biden had a point in mind for the 28-minute commencement address he delivered in 2021 at the Coast Guard Academy in New London, Connecticut.

- But if he did, it was his little secret. And the graduates let him know it, with subdued reactions to his attempts at humor, including a Navy joke that flopped.

The president finally got a real laugh with an out-and-out insult. "You're a really dull class," he said, in apparent frustration and desperation. "I mean, come on, man. Is the sun getting to you?"

- And then, the most painful moment of all. You never want to have to say: "But all kidding aside . . ."

THE TAKEAWAY: President Biden didn't have a Big Thought he was excited to convey. He was reading a fine but forgettable speech. When the audience's attention wandered, so did his.

This is how President Biden tried to grab 'em:

- "The world is changing. We're at a significant inflection point in world history. And our country and the world—the United States of America has always been able to chart the future in times of great change. We've been able to constantly renew ourselves. And time and again, we've proven there's not a single thing we cannot do as a nation when we do it together—and I mean that—not a single solitary thing."

Jeez. Let me fix that for you, Mr. President:

- "Nice work, graduates. You're living in an epic time in world history—and you can make a massive, lasting difference, fast. Here's how . . ."

Foggy, groggy generalities versus short, sharp and punchy. No contest.

GETTING IT RIGHT: Some of the most spellbinding speeches in the world are TED Talks—taut remarks by an expert who has a Big Thought that's been refined by countless retellings.

- Here's a secret of TED, the nonprofit that sponsors these gems: Every talk is 18 minutes or less—no matter who you are.

- Chris Anderson, the head of TED, says that's "short enough to hold people's attention," but "long enough to say something that matters." Not a bad formula.

One of the most-viewed TED Talks ever is "How to Spot a Liar" by social-networking expert Pamela Meyer. She began her 2011 talk by saying: "I don't want to alarm anybody in this room, but it's just come to my attention that the person to your right is a liar."

- You've got my attention, Pamela. And all it took was one sentence.

Then she dropped a funny: "Ever since I wrote this book *Liespotting*, no one wants to meet me in person anymore, no, no, no, no, no. They say, 'It's OK, we'll email you.'"
That's good stuff. Two sentences.

- Then she gave a little map: "So before I get started, what I'm going to do is I'm going to clarify my goal for you."

- Then her Big Thought: "Lying is a cooperative act. . . . Its power emerges when someone else agrees to believe the lie."

Nailed it.

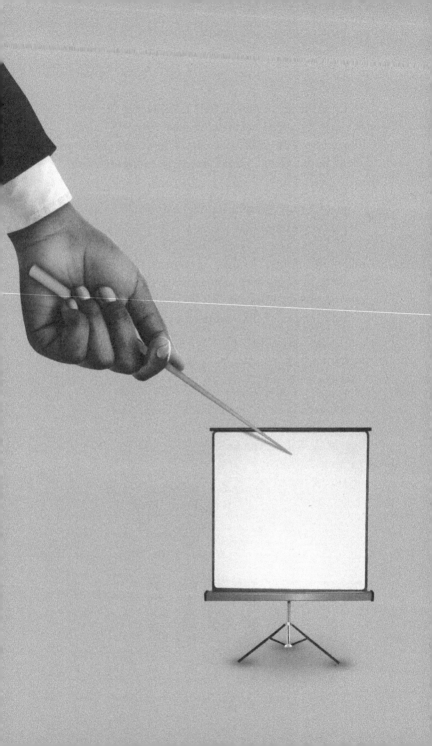

Smart Brevity
Your
Presentations

SMART BREVITY COUNT

710 WORDS	2½ MINUTES

So many presentations are stressful for the presenter, boring for the audience and a waste of time for both.

WHY IT MATTERS: Think of a PowerPoint masterpiece as minimalist. Nirvana is the fewest words, on the fewest slides, with the fewest distractions possible.

- You want everything you present to guide and amplify your most essential points—and never merely repeat or, worst of all, suck away attention and retention.

This is the opposite of your instincts and most of the NASCAR-like noise you suffer on Zoom or in meeting rooms.

- "Imagine a widely used and expensive prescription drug that claimed to make you beautiful but didn't," information design theorist Edward Tufte once said of PowerPoint. "Instead, the drug had frequent, serious side effects: making us stupid, degrading the quality and credibility of our communication, turning us into bores, wasting our colleagues' time. These side effects, and resulting unsatisfactory cost/benefit ratio, would rightly lead to a worldwide recall."

The world needs a PowerPoint intervention. Be the change, sisters and brothers. Start simple:

- You can talk, you can use slides, you can show pretty pictures. None of it matters if you don't have a crystal-clear idea of what you want the audience to remember.

- It's like a newsletter, email, speech, tweet or any other way you communicate: *Think before you PowerPoint.*

- Hone your idea so you know exactly—strong word for strong word—what you're saying and "Why it matters."

There is a guiding principle that applies to all communications, but to presentations in particular: Simplify to exaggerate. Think fewer words, fewer slides, fewer visuals—destroy anything that distracts from the *essential* points. Then, put into practice these specific presentation hacks:

1. Write down the precise outcome you want and three to five points you MUST make to support it.

- Put your supporting points in order as if you were arguing a case before a jury. This is your outline.

- Apply the Smart Brevity writing tricks to sharpen your specific ask or outcome into six or so words. This focuses the audience's mind on THE most important point.

2. Simplify every slide.

- One message per slide. People should absorb your point in 3 seconds, max. Think of each slide as a billboard: Would someone racing by at 65 miles per hour get the point?

- Research shows text is one of the least effective ways to communicate in a presentation. So minimize it.

- Stick with one font and/or one common visual style.

3. Pictures tell a vivid story. They are exponentially more effective than clumps of words. Combine pictures with a few words—attention and retention will soar.

What's happening?

- Neurologists say that when we're taking in new information, our brains can process a maximum of two stimuli—say, spoken word and pictures. But throw a bunch of bulleted text on top of that? You've lost me. Read from slides? Forget about it—your audience sure has.

- Molecular biologist John Medina found that images = lasting recall. He discovered that adding an arresting image can increase recall to 65 percent, compared to 10 percent if a person simply hears it.

4. Keep it short, stupid. Educational theory shows we can process a presentation best if it has one big idea, backed by three to five points. It's like Smart Brevity anywhere else.

- Talk to friends who work on Wall Street and you'll hear crazy tales of how many late-night hours go into fancy presentation decks that do absolutely nothing to inform, persuade or motivate.

- The *Harvard Business Review* says a partner at McKinsey tells new hires to use this rule of thumb: For every 20 slides you want to put in your deck, use 2.

Great advice. Just cut it down—a dozen, total, should suffice.

- Fewer words, images, transitions and sounds will all make your presentation sharper and more memorable.

5. Always be closing. Like any salesperson worth their salt, you won't get what you want without specifically and directly asking for it. Just fill in the blank:

I called this meeting and created this deck so I can get _____ or teach you _____.

- This, distilled into as few words as humanly possible, is your final slide.

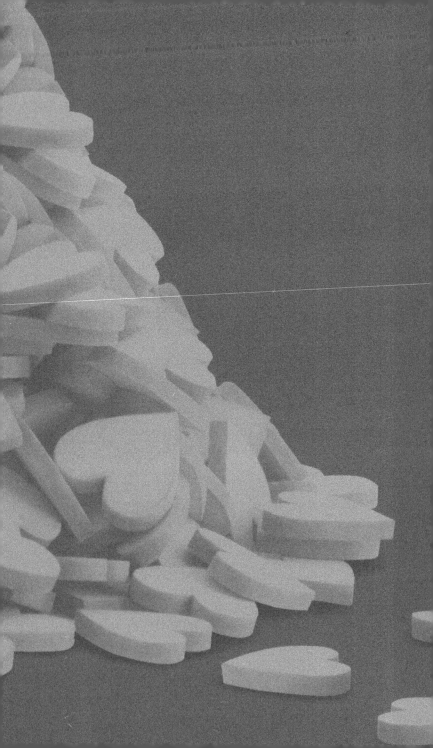

19

Smart Brevity Your Social Media

SMART BREVITY COUNT

433	2
WORDS	MINUTES

Social media is the hand-to-hand combat of attention warfare.

WHY IT MATTERS: There's no more Darwinian setting in communications than when you're scrolling a social feed. In an email, you have a few seconds to grab someone's attention. On Twitter or Instagram, it's the blink of an eye.

- The efficient cleanliness of Smart Brevity helps your social posts pop amid the chaotic clutter of Twitter, Facebook, Instagram. You're more likely to burst through, get a click or share, win attention.

- A+ tweet: "🌙 –> Moon's wet."

- Blah tweet—the lede of the story: "There is water on the moon's surface, and ice may be widespread in its many shadows, according to a pair of studies published Monday in the journal *Nature Astronomy*."

A winning formula for most social media posts is giving something to the audience—an idea, a score, a laugh—rather than asking them to click, buy or do something.

- If you're giving the reader something, they're more likely to engage with your content, and the algorithms will begin to reward you.

We've talked a lot about thinking of the one thing you want to tell a reader or listener—the one thing you want them to remember.

- On social media, you're ONLY going to tell them that one thing. Tease them with a newsy nugget. Provoke them with a surprising quote. Wow them with a memorable data point.

- Social media forces us to be ruthlessly selective. No matter how awesome your idea or prose, Twitter, Instagram and Facebook will ration what gets seen on a given card.

1 **Know your audience.**

- Twitter likes facts, data, a hot quote, a news break—the more urgent, the better.

- Instagram is changing. It used to be fancy photos, all filtered up. Now more people are getting news and information from Instagram. The winning formula here is an eye-catching image, with a side of slim, muscular text. Since you often can't link out to a post, Insta forces you to boil it down.

- If Twitter is jumpy and Insta is cool, Facebook is hot. You get action and traction here by putting a provocative spin on your idea or announcement. If it's a snore, it'll vanish without a trace under the crashing waves of the News Feed.

2 **Be image conscious.**

Pick clean, simple, arresting images to pull in your audience. All three are visual platforms—Twitter the least so—but words without art are a loser everywhere.

3 **Bust out your Smart Brevity writing and emoji moves.**

Every trick—from strong, simple words to evocative emojis—works in most social situations, if done right.

SMART BREVITY IN ACTION

Smart Brevity
Your
Visuals

SMART BREVITY COUNT

| 537 WORDS | 2 MINUTES |

Hopefully the simple, arresting art atop each chapter shows you how Smart Brevity applies to creative.

WHY IT MATTERS: At Axios, we aspire to what we call "elegant efficiency." When we design art for our website, newsletters and marketing materials, we obsess about one thing: What's the cleanest, sharpest, most pleasing way to display it?

- Establishing hierarchy and being reader-first should guide your design just like it does your writing, explains Sarah Grillo, our in-house visuals expert.

Hierarchy is a fundamental idea in art and design in which the elements of a visual are assigned importance through the use of scale, color and contrast to guide the viewer's eye. This is similar to how hierarchy is established in Smart Brevity writing.

- For examples, see how every chapter in this book starts: a brief opening line introducing an idea, supported by some form of "Why it matters."

- Good hierarchy often goes unnoticed. Poor hierarchy draws unwanted attention.

To put readers first, all visuals must be considered through the lens of how readers will interpret them. Ask yourself:

- Does the concept make sense to someone seeing it with fresh eyes?

- Are all the elements legible?

- How well does the layout express your content?

The headline and story may not even be necessary to understand the concept a strong illustration is communicating.

THE TAKEAWAY: To achieve Smart Brevity in visuals, follow this formula:

- Start with a strong concept.

- Edit out superfluous elements.

- Always judge the work from the perspective of the viewer.

Below is an example from an Axios story, titled "Texas Republicans Admit There's a Problem," about the retirement of six Texas House Republicans. The concept

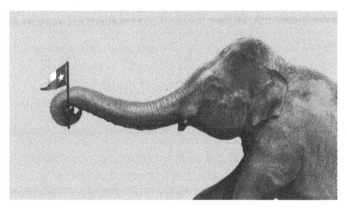

was to show an elephant waving a tiny flag of Texas, alluding to holding up a flag in defeat.

This illustration works, but the flag is dwarfed by the elephant. In terms of establishing hierarchy, the first place you look is at the head of the elephant. The flag becomes an afterthought. It's also small in comparison to the elephant and might be tricky for some readers to see.

WHY IT WORKS: Scaling up the elements and cropping out the majority of the elephant is transformational. Now there's balance between the elements and a stronger sense of hierarchy. The superfluous element was the body of the elephant. The vast negative space of the background also helps balance the illustration more successfully than in the first iteration.

You can see a similar dynamic at play with the design of our mobile-site pages and newsletter items—what we call a "screen." We obsessed over every pixel, spending months creating the most pleasing possible page, rather than the packed, dizzying screen you're used to.

SARAH'S TIPS & TRICKS

1 **Grab people with the visuals and words you choose.**

This applies to PowerPoint presentations or projects at school.

2 **Be direct—in art, design and language.**

3 **Create a hierarchy to guide your intended audience.**

Make sure the most important visual cue captures the eye of the reader.

4 **Offer context.**

This can be in color, depth or visual setting.

5 **Be respectful of your audience— abstraction, clutter, confusion are the enemy.**

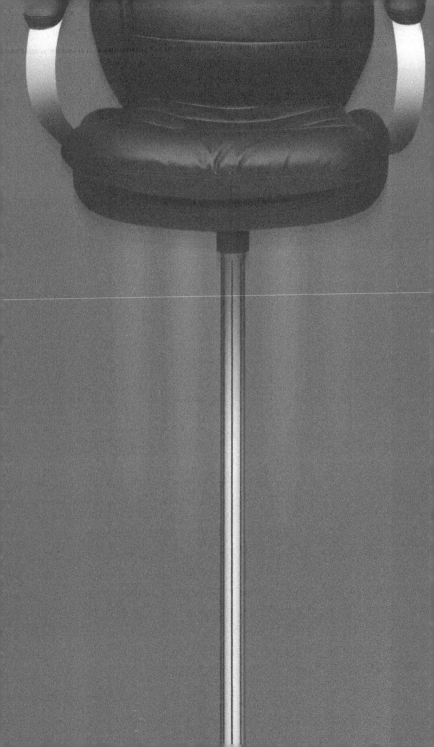

How to Run a Company on Smart Brevity

This would be a stupid, waste-of-time book if we didn't practice what we preach. We run our entire company on Smart Brevity.

WHY IT MATTERS: It's central to our management and culture and a big reason we win awards for having an inclusive, happy, kick-ass workplace.

GO DEEPER: Axios is currently a more than 500–person start-up with a lively, hyper-ambitious, insanely transparent culture. Every employee owns equity in Axios, and we'll answer *any* question, with two exceptions—how much someone makes and why someone left. We stay silent on those two out of respect for individual privacy.

- **FUN FACT:** We allow every employee to ask anything anonymously—absolutely anything— and read the question verbatim in a weekly meeting, no matter how blunt or rude, then answer it. Yes, this can be awkward.

A magical thing happens when you communicate crisply and transparently: You cut out all the employee gossip and pot-stirring that come from being confused or kept in the dark.

We tell leaders and friends from other companies and in our personal lives that their right-hand person should be a communicator, not an operator or money whiz. The public, employees, shareholders, investors and friends all demand to know what you're doing and why you're doing it.

- Communications failures can cripple or confuse an entire organization.

THE BIG PICTURE: We're all communicators now. Never have humans talked, tweeted or texted more words—and found it more difficult to be heard. So you better be good at it, or find someone who is.

- Our staff, like all others, demands to know what we stand for and why we do the things we do. Most executives suck at providing these answers.

- Remote and hybrid working make quick, clear communications exponentially more urgent and important. How can a salesperson working in Oshkosh, Wisconsin, stay inspired and connected to bosses in NYC without it?

- The Project Management Institute found that 30 percent of project failures stemmed from crappy communications. It is usually where things break down for us when we stumble.

- Most people leaving their jobs point to feelings of disconnectedness and fading engagement, according to Edelman polling.

AXIOS IN-HOUSE NEWSLETTERS

Lights On from our revenue team . . . *Cranes* from Axios Local . . . *Click Clack* from our web-traffic guru . . . *The Funnel* from our head of growth . . . *The TopLine* from our sales warriors.

- Those are just a few of the newsletters regularly published by Axios execs using Axios HQ—for their bosses, their teams and their colleagues across the company.

WHY IT MATTERS: This gives winners a forum for sharing best practices, encourages healthy competition among business units and gets rid of silos—everyone has visibility on what everyone's up to.

BETWEEN THE LINES: For the cofounders, these updates are an early-warning system for anyone's activities that might be veering away from company goals. In one Sunday evening, we can be sure everyone's on track and spot pockets that need our attention, encouragement or kudos.

- And here's our favorite part: When we have one-on-one meetings with our leaders, we're already caught up. So we can use that time to talk through innovations, insights, bottlenecks, disruptions.

ZOOM IN: Popular content in these updates includes most-read newsletter subject lines, sneak peeks at new products and revenue milestones.

- As "1 fun thing" at the end, people include what they're reading or listening to, pictures of their dogs, stats from a team member's marathons. In these work-from-everywhere times, it's a new chance to get to know a colleague you may never meet in person.

THE TAKEAWAY: The communications crisis isn't confined to business or top leaders. The more noise and distractions there are, the more precision and efficiency matter in being heard—and remembered in all things.

- Just look at politics. Power no longer flows from position, seniority or money. It flows to those who master—or game—modern, short-burst communications on cable news or Twitter.

- Teachers, preachers, small-group leaders—everyone who communicates one-to-many—face similar challenges in penetrating brains snapped around by quick-twitch technology.

This is another thing we learned the hard way. At Politico, in our early days, we scoffed at communications and culture and figured everything would be fine if people just did their jobs.

We were dead wrong. Our attrition rate was so high, *The New Republic*, a national magazine, wrote that our company was "a punishing place to work." We had to change, starting with more transparent and regular conversations with the staff.

- We are beating the dealer on this one now at Axios by communicating internally the way we communicate with readers. It started with what we call *5 Big Things*— a weekly newsletter, all in Smart Brevity, that details in order of importance what we're thinking or doing. It is blunt, fun and essential.

Jim writes it every Sunday with a more than massive assist from our Chief of Staff, Kayla Brown, the soul of our enterprise. She had already been doing a Friday update when she said we should do all our communications this way. And so *5 Big Things* was born.

Roy had the genius idea of having every executive do the same thing for their team—and share it with their fellow executives. Now every week, every executive knows every big thing in order of importance. We eliminated canned updates in meetings, and no one says: "I didn't know we're doing that!" We just jump in and get to what's next.

- Stay informed: By the time Jim sits down to write on Sunday, he knows everything important going on in the company. We joke that he could run the company from his fishing boat in Maine. The reality: Kayla often *does* from her childhood home in Kerrville, Texas.

But the biggest beneficiaries are the employees. We all hate to be out of the loop, baffled about direction, confused about purpose. Now our company leaders send us emails in Smart Brevity—just as the BP staff did after Geoff Morrell introduced it—and start their own newsletters to organize people around their passions.

THE RUNDOWN

Matt Burns, who's worked in political and corporate communications for 20 years, said it's one of the great mysteries of our time: People's consumption habits have evolved, but communication hasn't. Burns— head of communications at GRAIL, a Silicon Valley biotech company focused on early cancer detection, now with Scipher Medicine in Boston—said the big struggle now is how to get and keep people's attention.

- He set out to strangle one of the biggest internal time-killers: ad-hoc emails.

Burns started using our Axios HQ software while working at UnitedHealth Group and immediately made it the central part of his strategy when he jumped to GRAIL and then Scipher. He needed to quickly and instantly align the scattered, speedy start-ups as they pounded out new products.

- Burns found that, especially for reaching the company's younger scientists, efficiency is paramount: "They open their email and take a quick look."

- "Every minute counts in their work," Burns told us. "They don't have spare time to search for information to remain connected to the company's broader priorities and culture—they need information delivered succinctly and predictably."

To cut down on all those random emails at GRAIL, Burns started a weekly newsletter, *The Rundown*.

- It shows up like clockwork in all 750-plus employees' inboxes, "just like the old afternoon or morning paper," according to Burns.

- The cheery opening: "It's Friday, GRAILERers!" 🎉 Each issue is about 1,400 words—a 5-minute read.

Now Burns's colleagues lobby him to get their items included.

- GRAIL's countless random internal emails were often opened by fewer than one-third of recipients. The more dependable, efficient newsletters have open rates of around 90 percent. A similar newsletter Burns established at Scipher already has open rates over 75 percent after only a few months.

1 Mission matters.

Find ways to pull your items back to the soul and purpose of your organization. "Why it matters" is the perfect device.

- It is impossible to overdose on this: Your mission begins to sink in only when you've annoyed yourself with repetition.

2 Tell a story.

If someone read all of your newsletters from the previous year, they should tell a clear, powerful story about what you were doing, thinking, accomplishing. Each item or each newsletter should do the same.

- People bore easily. They want an authentic story to explain why they work so hard and bother reading your words.

- We give new employees a copy of the previous few months of *5 Big Things* so they can hit the ground running.

3 Don't be a fraud.

Write with candor and authenticity. People aren't suckers—they can sniff out a lawyered line or constipated corporate nonsense. Quit doing this ASAP.

4 Don't quit.

You need to connect with your staff at least once a week. Resist the urge to blow off the newsletter. If you don't want others to slack off, lead by example.

5 Be humble.

If you're a CEO, leader or manager, you're successful and hopefully smart. But not *that* smart. Show gratitude, admit mistakes, poke fun at yourself. It frees those around you to stop acting like self-important corporate jackasses too.

6 Encourage copycats.

The magic really unfolds when those around you start communicating in the same style and similar cadence. Once we realized Smart Brevity was a game-changer *within* Axios as well as for our outside audience, we saw a spike in alignment among teams. Everyone has fun telling their own story and knows what colleagues are up to—throughout the company and around the country.

Communicate
Inclusively

SMART BREVITY COUNT

| 991 WORDS | 3 ½ MINUTES |

If you're not communicating inclusively, you're not communicating effectively.

WHY IT MATTERS: We're talking about being accessible, relatable and credible with everyone in your audience—regardless of gender, race, color, religion, gender identity, age, physical ability, sexual orientation or anything else.

- The principles of Smart Brevity can help bridge differences in background and abilities. It's direct and stripped down—accessible and nondivisive by design.

- Executed carefully, it's a universal style of communication, naturally cleansing much of the cultural bias and complexity from the author.

- It can make what matters most accessible to people with learning disabilities—such as dyslexia— and those for whom English is a second language. We live in a diverse country in a globalized time, so these principles are more important than ever.

THE WAY TO WIN: Know you have blind spots, be aware of them and take steps to be sure you're uplifting diverse voices.

- Case in point: Axios was started by three white dudes. There are lots of life experiences we're missing—and lots of perspectives we need to be very deliberate about seeking out.

- At Axios, we made diversity, equity and inclusion a priority from Day One, both in hiring and in the people who are around our decision-making table.

Think about your own blind spots, which can be based on any of the considerations we mentioned here, or on geography, ideology, birthplace, income or . . . you can't list them all.

- Then, if you're writing something sensitive or overly complicated or anything really, run it by someone who's had different experiences than you or who has lived a different life than you have.

Here, from the Axios newsroom, are some best practices for inclusive writing:

- **BE SPECIFIC** when writing about someone. Ask them how they identify: Asian American, Chinese American, etc. When referring to Indigenous Americans, indicate their tribe when possible. And don't forget to confirm their preferred gender pronouns.

- **CUT DESCRIPTORS** that may subtly reinforce stereotypes of people or communities. Consult resources like the Conscious Style Guide (https://consciousstyleguide.com) to learn about language to avoid.

- **DIG DEEPER** into photo choices to avoid facilitating tropes, like illustrating #StopAsianHate by showing Asian takeout places.

This tip is gold:

- **SWAP** one identity for another—one race or ethnicity for another, one nationality for another—and see if the language and intention of the sentence remain nonjudgmental.

Here is another area where Smart Brevity is your friend: We often can avoid pitfalls by simply omitting irrelevant information. The Asian American Journalists Association tells us:

- **"IS RACE/ETHNICITY/RELIGION/NATIONAL ORIGIN RELEVANT?** . . . Using the descriptors when they're not relevant or without explaining their relevance perpetuates harmful stereotypes."

Sharp, clear writing can go a long way in preventing offense. When we read these guidelines from the National Center on Disability and Journalism, we realized these are just good rules for writing—period:

- **"REFER TO A DISABILITY** only when it's relevant to the story and, when possible, confirm the diagnosis with a reputable source, such as a medical professional or other licensed professional."

- **"WHEN POSSIBLE**, ask sources how they would like to be described. If the source is not available or unable to communicate, ask a trusted family member, advocate, medical professional or relevant organization that represents people with disabilities."

GO DEEPER: The style guide of the National Association of Black Journalists is organized alphabetically to help with specific terms.

- Just browsing the entries reminded us of how different people can hear words and phrases in very different ways.

THE BOTTOM LINE: Offend me or confuse me and you've lost me. Not just for this newsletter or presentation, but for good.

- Case in point: One in five children report learning disabilities, according to the National Center for Learning Disabilities. If this holds true into adulthood, you are talking about 65 million Americans. So, this could be 20 percent of your audience.

1 Write in plain, clear language:

This allows people to better understand the message you are trying to share. It's about making sure words are crisp and clear and anyone can understand them. Using this rule not only helps people with learning disabilities but also helps people who speak and read English as a second language.

2 Use bullet points:

Businesspeople love bullet points, and Roy has been using them to communicate clearly since business school. They force you to figure out the most important points and separate them into their components. Too often, people mix several points together—and lose their audience.

3 Keep it simple—and short:

Complexity confuses. Abstraction alienates. Length loses. You can unite people around a common understanding of an important idea or update by writing in short, direct sentences and by losing the clever insider-isms or fancy clauses.

Roy recalls that in college and at work, "I started to see I was very different from other people. Dyslexia caused great pain in my life, but it gave me a gift. I had to problem-solve, work harder, create systems to thrive."

BOTTOM LINE: We did not create Smart Brevity for people with learning or language challenges—or to promote inclusivity per se. But, watching it in action, it helps with all three.

ROY'S STORY

The teachers in the town of Ilford in Essex, England, thought Roy was a problem child. They made him feel dumb and difficult. His spelling was often atrocious. His grades sagged.

- His seventh-grade English class at Ilford County High School for boys was a real gut punch—one he would remember and recount in a speech for kids with learning disabilities three decades later. He got back a paper with yet another lackluster grade, filled with red lines and comments.

- "Short and not very sweet," the teacher scribbled. "Do you not own a dictionary?"

He was not dumb. Roy was dyslexic. (Yes, you should feel like an ass if you're Roy's teacher reading this.)

The Cheat Sheet

SMART BREVITY COUNT

| 724 WORDS | 3 MINUTES |

Here's a quick-and-easy guide to doing
Smart Brevity yourself.

GUIDING PRINCIPLES

AUTHORITY:

You are a trustworthy source of information, and
only an expert can understand an issue, evaluate
what's new or important and distill it in an accurate,
interesting way.

Be the expert, or find one.

BREVITY:

You stand out for being respectful of busy readers'
time, giving them exactly what they need to stay
productive, without leaving them hungry or
unfulfilled.

Stay short, not shallow.

WHY IT MATTERS: Think of this as your entry-level class. Do it a few times and watch how quickly your brain adapts to doing it intuitively.

HUMANITY:

You can communicate with the full spectrum of human emotion, sophistication and nuance but challenge yourself to present your message in a way that's familiar and conversational.

Write like you speak.

CLARITY:

You should be frugal with words for the sake of brevity so that what you ultimately present to readers is approachable, clear and simple to scan in a realistic amount of time.

Style text for impact.

Define your audience.

- Specify what you want them to know

Fill in the prompts below (60 seconds or less)

WHO is the smart reader for this exercise?

WHAT is an update or other topic you're familiar with
and they need to know about:

WHY is it significant? Jot down a few details.
We'll come back to them later:

Structure it—smartly and succinctly

- Visualize what you want the output to be. In most cases, the art will be optional.

HEADLINE:
Is it . . .

- 6 words or fewer?
- Clear and specific?
- Conversational, with muscular words?

WHAT'S NEW:
Is it . . .

- One sentence only?
- What you need readers to remember?
- A distinct detail from your headline?

Fill in the prompts below (30 seconds or less)

WRITE your headline and first sentence—remember the tips and tricks.

Example:

BEFORE	AFTER
UPDATE ON OUR WORK-FROM-HOME PLANS IN 2021	**🏠 REMOTE WORK OPTION EXTENDED**
We continue to closely monitor the impact of COVID, and we are writing today to provide an update on our plans for the rest of the year.	**Everyone will have the option—but not the requirement—to work from home for the rest of 2021.**

Explain the significance and context

- Write the words "Why it matters," bold them and slap a colon at the end.

- Think about the person you listed as your target audience.

- In one sentence, explain the reason you are sharing this with them as bluntly and briefly as possible.

Come up with your own unique axioms

- Think about your industry, personality, brand, voice and tone.

BRAINSTORM a better version of each of these Axioms so they resonate with your audience.

Fill in the prompts below (60 seconds or less)

SMART BREVITY   YOUR VERSIONS

WHAT'S NEXT:

THE BOTTOM LINE:

BY THE NUMBERS:

THE BIG PICTURE:

Use your Axioms to provide intros to any other essential info.

- Break any clumps of data or related points into bullet points.

Review your work.

- At this point you have a pretty tidy piece of writing, scripting or other communication. It's focused with a priority reader in mind, the top is structured to pull in your audience and the body is styled to boost scannability and keep readers moving.

The last few checks we do are the ones likely also familiar to you:

- **ACCURATE**: Confirm that you didn't lose necessary detail or *essential* nuance during your editing process. If you did, bring it back.

- **COHESIVE**: Make sure everything still flows. Sometimes elements like transitional phrases get cut for the sake of brevity, but at the end, if your communication feels disjointed, reintroduce the more important of those.

- **HUMAN**: Most important, make sure there's still a sense of voice and personality in your update. The first few times you use Smart Brevity, if your communication feels curt or overly cut, you've gone too far. Take a minute to breathe a little bit of life back into your text.

- You will sound sharp, efficient, real—and be heard again. A one-to-many communication that should feel a lot shorter, smarter and authentic.

WHY IT MATTERS: We are confident you will discover what we have discovered. These tips and tricks will help you win the war for attention—and make you be heard again.

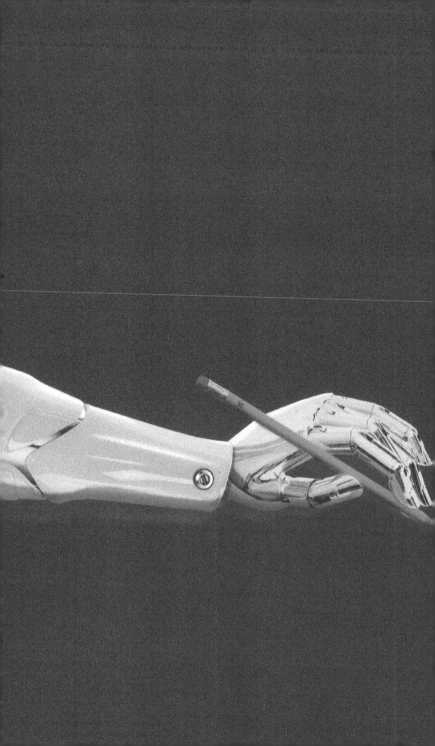

24

Take Smart Brevity for a Spin

If you've made it this deep into the book, you're miles ahead of your friends and competitors: You realize that you'll lose—or get lost—if you don't rethink and retool how you communicate.

WHY IT MATTERS: This is your chance to test-drive Smart Brevity and see how much you learned— and where you can sharpen your skills.

Go to
SmartBrevity.com,
upload your writing
and see how
it scores!

- Go to SmartBrevity.com, upload something you wrote, and get an instant Smart Brevity score and some helpful feedback. You could do this a couple of times to see if your Smart Brevity score goes up over time.

If you want to implement Smart Brevity in your organization, company, school, nonprofit, team or division then visit SmartBrevity.com. We have helpful videos, case studies and information on how you can implement this across an organization to help you communicate more effectively.

THE BIG PICTURE: Hundreds of companies, nonprofits and government offices use Axios HQ and have seen overnight improvement in the response to updates they send to their internal teams and outside audiences. Think of it as Next Level Smart Brevity.

1. Templates: Axios HQ has dozens of formats for a weekly all-hands newsletter to a sales team, investors or board update.

2. Smart Brevity Score: Our AI gives your writing a numerical score so you can optimize your writing before you send—and see your improvement.

3. Smart Brevity Guidance: As you type, tips pop up to suggest better words, stronger structures, the perfect heading. The bot flags headlines that are long and passages that are too wordy.

4. Collaboration: Our software lets you invite several people to work together on these updates—and even assign certain sections to people so they can quickly and easily fill in their part.

5. Analytics: See who opened your newsletter and when. This shows you with real data what truly engages people.

6. A living history: These updates become a handy library to let new members of the team catch up and speak your language.

OUR FINAL THOUGHT: We hope all these tools and tricks in this book allow you to break through the noise, communicate with renewed confidence and be heard again.

Acknowledgments

Smart Brevity was the vision of the authors when we started Axios with three people and no name. In the five years since, Smart Brevity has been stress-tested and refined by the now 150-plus journalists of Axios and the huge team building our software service, Axios HQ, which brings Smart Brevity superpower to companies and organizations.

WHY IT MATTERS: Smart Brevity is empowering. If you follow this book's precepts—starting with the importance of honing your idea before you begin typing—you'll be able to communicate with authority and impact.

Massive shoutout to Kayla Brown, Axios Employee No. 1, now chief of staff of Axios. There would be no book without her. She has consistently managed and optimized the magic of putting our secret sauce between covers.

With a special thanks to:

Autumn VandeHei, the better half of Jim and the true words maestro.

And **Kelly Schwartz**, the better half of Roy and the backbone of Smart Brevity.

Rafe Sagalyn, one of Washington's most sought-after book agents, who had the first vision for "Smart Brevity" the book.

The team at Workman, a legendary publishing house, for believing in the project from the very first Zoom, then deploying formidable expertise from across the company to help us stick our landing.

Thank you to our entire Axios family. This book could not have happened without the magic you create every day.

With a special thanks to these folks that went above and beyond in bringing this book to life: Aïda Amer, Sara Fischer, Qian Gao, Justin Green, Sarah Grillo, Sara Kehaulani Goo, Tristyn Hassani, Emily Inverso, Nicholas Johnston, Danielle Jones, David Nather, Neal Rothschild, Alison Snyder, Jordan Zaslav.

And to the friends of Axios we interviewed for the book or leaned on for research support: Eddie Berenbaum, Matt Burns, Jon Clifton and the Gallup team, Jamie Dimon, India Dunn, Megan Green, Anna Greenberg and Jason Ashley, Elizabeth Lewis, Alice Lloyd, Geoff Morrell, Lisa Osborne Ross, Mark Smith, Ronald Yaros, Chris Sims, and John Bresnahan.

Would you like your people to read this book?

If you would like to discuss how you could bring these ideas to your team, we would love to hear from you. Our titles are available at competitive discounts when purchased in bulk across both physical and digital formats. We can offer bespoke editions featuring corporate logos, customized covers, or letters from company directors in the front matter can also be created in line with your special requirements.

We work closely with leading experts and organizations to bring forward-thinking ideas to a global audience. Our books are designed to help you be more successful in work and life.

For further information, or to request a catalogue, please contact:
business@johnmurrays.co.uk

Nicholas Brealey Publishing is an imprint of
John Murray Press.